Metal Trading

Comprehensive Beginner's Guide to Get Started and Learn Metal Trading from A-Z

TABLE OF CONTENTS

Introduction

Metal is an incredible all-round material that is used in countless applications. Its use ranges from construction to electronics due to the numerous qualities it possesses. In this book, we will give you a complete guide on what metal is and how to trade it. We have come up with a comprehensive guide that will answer all your questions about the trading of this highly valued material.

Metals in its pure form comes naturally from the earth's crust. Because it is combined with a rock and other minerals, they usually take the form of ore, therefore the ore needs to be extracted so that it can be separated from the rock.

However, in the case of metals like gold, the extractions are sometimes done by elements. This explains why it is possible to see gold in river beds because the water movement has already caused their movement by breaking the rock.

Common Properties of Metals

There are a variety of minerals that hold different properties, making metal ideal for various applications. Below are some of the common features of metals:

- Hard
- Have a high melting point
- High tensile strength
- They are lustrous
- They are good conductors of both heat and electricity
- Have high density

It is important to note that different metals have different levels of properties. For example, when it comes to hardness, potassium and lithium are very soft and can easily be cut with a knife. On the other hand, chromium and titanium are tough metals that are very strong.

Let's begin so that you can learn more about this incredible material and how to trade it more effectively.

Chapter 1

What Makes Metals Important?

Metals are compounds, elements or alloys that are usually hard in their solid state. Typically, they are characterized by a shiny appearance, thermal and electrical conductivity, fusibility and malleability. Most of the elements in the periodic table are metals. Although we usually think of metals in their finished form that we see in products, the origin of metals starts from beneath the earth's surface.

Some elements like iron and aluminum are found in large quantities in the crust of the earth whereas others like gold and palladium are found in small amounts. However, enormous energy is required to produce even the most common elements from the earth's crust.

Metal's physical properties makes it ideal to be used as a raw material for the building and manufacturing industries for most of the important products that we use in our everyday lives. For instance, the construction industry will use metals to build homes, offices, airports, bridges, and railway lines. The manufacturing sector will use metals to make electronics, factory equipment, jewelry, medical equipment, cutlery, automobiles, and many other essential types of equipment.

Below is a compiled list of the use of metals in our daily lives:

In medicine: metals are found in our bodies as micro-elements. They help in the conduction of nerve impulses, carry oxygen through the blood, help facilitate the reactions of enzymes, and many more functions. Therefore, metals are used to heal any form of micronutrient metal deficiency disease in both humans and animals. For example, iron is a component of hemoglobin (HB) in the blood cells in the body and for that, it helps cure some form of anemia when used as ferrous sulfate.

Generally, almost all metals contain micro-essentials known as trace elements in our bodies. They form part of a few enzymes and co-enzymes. They are found in trace quantities in plants and animals. Typical examples of such metals include; magnesium (Mg), potassium (K), sodium (Na), and many more. Additionally, metals like aluminum, titanium, and magnesium are used as medicine to treat acid problems in the stomach. They are learned under the subject of inorganic chemistry.

Finally, most of the tools used in medicine like scissors, needles, scalpels and surgical blades are all made from metals. They are ideal due to their toughness and also because they can be sterilized at extreme temperatures.

In jewelry: a variety of metals are used to make jewelry. Knowing the different kinds of metals and their different benefits in making jewelry will help you make an informed decision on the kind of metal that you will trade. Commonly used metals to make jewelry include platinum, gold, titanium, silver, tungsten and stainless steel.

In electronics – electronics can be defined as equipment that depend primarily on electric power to function. Commonly used electronics include mobile phones, fridges, televisions, shaving machines, dry cleaners, etc.. All these equipment have metals as part of their structure, and it is used for different purposes. However, the primary goal of metal in electrical gadgets is to enhance the movement of electrical power. Most metals are good conductors, but the most used metals for conduction are copper and lead. It is true that without metals, electronics could not have progressed much. Thermocouples make it possible to automatically switch refrigerators and air conditioners on and off.

In building and construction: most metals, especially iron and steel are used to build homes and for construction. They are mainly used in reinforcing concrete roofs, pillars, foundations, and fencing among other uses during construction.

In the kitchen and for cooking: most utensils and other equipment used in the kitchen are made from metals such as aluminum, steel and copper. Things like bowls, spoons, knives, stoves and furnaces are all made from metal. These metallic tools are highly recommended due to their ability to withstand even the highest temperatures, and they can also be used for the dry and wet purpose.

In machinery and automobiles: most machines and motors are exclusively made from metals, and those that can withstand high temperatures and pressure while working are most preferred. Iron, aluminum and steel are commonly used for cranes, mills and satellites. The machines and automobiles used by these metals include vehicles, airplanes, ships, rockets and many more machines.

Additionally, these materials are the only recommended materials to help transport and store gas under pressure. Cylinders and tanks are made from metals to store and to transport gas when the need arises.

Use as furniture: some furniture in our homes are made from metal instead of wood. This includes stands, fans, cupboards, drawers, beds, etc. which are all are mainly made from metals.

In farming: farming requires many tools made of metal. We need metal tools to till the soil, for cutting, plowing, when planting, etc. the good thing is that metals tools can be used in all weather conditions.

In security systems: metals play a vital role in putting up security systems. Most metals are used to make things like safes, locks, cupboards to keep valuable items, etc. which are all essential for enhanced security. They play a significant role in preventing theft or misplacement.

In improving security: metal trade plays an essential role in the development of an economy. Most people will invest in bullion market and metal stock exchange and make a fortune. Since the demand for metals is on the rise, some traders consider it as the safest option for investment. Many countries depend on mineral export and especially metals for their economic growth.

Aside from the beneficial uses of metal that we have seen above, tungsten is a different kind of metal that is used to generate a stable light in electric bulbs and tubes. Tungsten is used over other types of metals because it can resist high temperatures that would arise as a result of electrical resistance. Additionally, mercury, which comes as a liquid at room temperatures is found in thermometers to help record daily temperatures. It is most preferred due to its ability to contact and expand after a small change in temperature. Today, due to the many common uses of metals, there is the development of metallurgy, a separate division of science and technology to help further explore the better combinations of metals and their uses.

Types of Metals

Metals are typically grouped in two categories: precious metals and base metals.

Precious Metals

Precious metals are rare and occur naturally as metallic elements with a high economic value. They are unique because they are both investments and industrial elements.

Manufacturers use precious metals to make jewelry, catalytic converters, electric components and dental equipment, among other items. Investors engage in collecting bars and coins made from precious metals, creating intense betting in commodity markets. Traders of precious metals view them as a perfect store of value compared to having printed money.

The precious metals in active commodities include:

- Gold
- Silver
- Platinum
- Palladium

Base Metals

Base metals are used in a variety of industries and commercial applications like construction and manufacturing. Their widespread daily use makes them important commodities in global markets. Some popular base metals include the following:

- Lead
- Aluminum
- Iron
- Copper
- Nickel
- Steel
- Molybdenum
- Zinc
- Tin

Chapter 2

What To Know Before Trading Metals Used In Jewelry

Below, you will find compiled information about each of these metals and how each suits a particular kind of jewelry.

Gold

Gold remains the most preferred metal to make earrings, pendants, fashion rings, necklaces, and bracelets. When it comes to gold, there are two critical things to look at. The first thing is its color, which can either be yellow or white, and the second thing is to know how many karats it has. The karats can either be 10k, 14k, or 18k. 14k karat is the most commonly used karat in the jewelry industry in the United States.

The level of karat in gold refers to the level of purity of gold comparing to other alloys used to produce the final metal. In the United States, K or Kt are the abbreviations for Karat, while some countries abbreviate it as Ct.

When trading gold, it is important to note that the higher the proportion of the metal, the more valuable it will be. Therefore, if all other things remain constant, an 18kt jewelry will cost more than a 14kt jewelry and equally a 14kt jewelry will be more expensive than a 10kt jewelry.

Jewelry with 10kt gold has 41.7% pure gold, 14k gold has 58.5% pure gold while 18k gold contains 75% pure gold.

The percentage that is not pure gold is made up of alloys. Alloys include various kinds of metals with the aim of giving the metal a unique appearance, like color. Jewelry is always marked with a stamp to show the kind of gold used.

Usually, a stamp for a 10kt will either be 416 or 417, 10kt or 10k. A stamp for a 14kt will either be number 585, 14kt or 14k, and for an 18kt, the mark will either be 750, 18kt or 18k. The marks only indicate the purity of metal, and its color. This means that you could have a 14k yellow ring stamped at 750 and also have a 14k white ring stamped at 750 too.

10k, 14k, and 18k gold are all relatively hard and durable metals which makes them suitable for all kinds of fine jewelry. Gold is especially preferred for jewelry that is worn on a daily basis. Most people will look at the hardness and durability of gold which will be used to make rings and other jewelry.

Image source – Pixabay.com

When looking to trade gold, it is important to know the difference between 10k and 18k gold. 10k is hard to bend and appears springier than 18k. For this reason, a ring made from 10k gold is less likely to bend out of shape than an 18k. However, it is worth noting that if the ring is well made, neither of the materials is likely to easily go out of shape.

- **What the color of gold means**

Gold comes in several different colors. The most common ones are yellow and white gold, followed by rose gold. Sometimes, there are gold colors available such as pink, red and green gold. Gold jewelry can also be made using combinations of different colors. This kind of jewelry is sometimes referred to as two-one, three-tone or multi-colored gold. The difference in color observed between yellow, white and rose is as a result of the metals used during the alloy mix. The difference in the color is caused by the kind of components used during the alloy mix and the yellow color of gold or rose will not fade away or wear off with time.

You can obtain the yellow color after you have mixed alloy metals of copper, zinc and silver. A rose color gold is obtained after mixing pure gold with alloys like copper. The copper gives it its rose-reddish color. White gold is obtained after mixing pure gold with white metals like nickel, tin, silver and palladium. In the past, nickel was used to make white gold. However, today, nickel is not used because it causes reactions in a lot of people.

Rhodium, a type of white metal found in the platinum family is used to coat white gold rings when they're new. It shares most of the platinum characters, such as its white color. The rhodium plate on the gold gives it a whiter look. The natural color of white gold is a result of the mix of a light gray color with traces of yellow. The yellow color in white gold originates from the pure gold used to make the metal alloy. Although rhodium is white and very hard, it does eventually wear out. In order to keep your white jewelry in its original color, you should re-apply the rhodium plate after around 6 to 18 months. This can be done at any local jeweler.

Sometimes, there is a difference in color between the different gold karats. For example, an 18k yellow gold piece will be more yellow than a 10k yellow gold one. Basically, an 18k piece will have a richer golden color. When it comes to the price of gold in the same karat, white gold prides itself as being the most expensive gold. Both yellow and rose gold cost almost the same.

If you are confused on how to choose between different karats of gold, consider the following:

- How the metal performs after being worn every day
- The color difference between 10k, 14k and 18k gold
- The price variation between the different gold karats

Practically, 14k and 18k jewelry tend to withstand everyday tear more than 10k gold jewelry. They also look better than 10k jewelry, even with time. This may be the reason why people looking for an engagement ring usually go for 14k or 18k gold rings. Below is a quick reference on the type of jewelry fit for gold:

Necklaces and bracelets – 14k gold

Fashion rings for men – 14k gold

Wedding rings for men – 14k or 18k gold

Wedding ring for ladies – 14k or 18k gold

Earrings and pendants – 14k gold

Colored stone ring for ladies – 14k 0r 18k gold

Sterling silver

Sterling silver metal is a white-grey metal that is relatively less expensive than gold, platinum and titanium. Silver is also a more soft metal than gold, titanium and platinum and does not possess the hardness of other metals. Sterling silver is usually 92.5% silver and is usually stamped at number 925.

Silver is commonly used in jewelry such as earrings, pendants, bracelets, necklaces and fashion rings. It is preferred for the kind of jewelry that is not usually worn on an everyday basis. This is why it is not recommended for men's or women's wedding rings and it is not suitable for ladies' engagement rings either.

Silver is prone to oxidation, and this may sometimes make it turn black. However, you can make the silver jewelry look like new again by using a silver jewelry cleaner that is available in hard stores or departments.

Platinum

Platinum is a kind of metal that naturally comes directly from the earth in white. Unlike gold, platinum has to be masked with other alloys to have the yellow color. Platinum is manufactured into jewelry that contains 90 or 95% pure platinum. Platinum jewelry is long lasting and extraordinarily white and you don't have to apply for a rhodium plate like in gold to give it its white color.

Platinum is a hefty and dense meal, so a platinum ring will be much heavier than even an 118k gold ring.

Availability of Platinum

Platinum is about 30 times rarer than gold. It is found in very few places around the world, like Canada, South America and Zimbabwe. In a single year, only 88 tons of platinum are made into jewelry, compared to 2,700 tons of gold made into jewelry each year. It takes about eight weeks to produce a single ounce (31.1 grams) of platinum. There are much fewer platinum mines than gold mines. The ratio of gold mines to platinum mines is 10:1.

Surprisingly, platinum is more expensive than gold. If all other things remain constant, a platinum ring will cost almost twice the cost of an 18k white gold ring. There are three reasons for this. First, as mentioned earlier, platinum is much denser, so a ring made of platinum will weigh more than an 18k ring. The cost of platinum is almost double the price of gold and, finally, platinum jewelry is 20-25% purer than 18k gold jewelry.

Platinum is a rich selection that is usually chosen due to its sophisticated appeal and its popularity among first class people.

Below are the purity levels of platinum and alloys used with platinum:

900 platinum has 95% pure platinum (900 parts in 1000 parts)

950 platinum has 95% pure platinum (950 parts in 1000 parts)

The alloys used with platinum include Cobalt, Palladium, Tungsten, Ruthenium and Iridium.

Just like gold, platinum is stamped and marked, indicating the type of platinum. For 950 platinum, the stamp will either be the number 950 or platinum, Pt or Plat, whereas for the 900 platinum, the stamp will either be the number 900 or platinum, Pt or Plat. It is rare for platinum to be used in a full range of jewelry products due to its cost and heavy weight. It is mostly used to make ladies' engagements rings and wedding rings for men. Platinum is also used to make fashion and colored rings; however, it is not commonly used to make earrings, bracelets, necklaces or pendants due to its weight.

Palladium

Palladium belongs to the platinum group of metals. It was first used to make jewelry after platinum was declared a strategic metal and was reserved for use by the military in 1939. Palladium alloys made for jewelry contain about 95% palladium and about 5% ruthenium and may comprise of other types of metals that relate to their developer. The 950 palladium are white in color, malleable, noble, lightweight, hypo allergic and have a smooth finish and polish. Importantly, they don't require rhodium plating and have a desirable, platinum-like setting and forming characteristics. The 950 palladium does not require the white color to be renewed through rhodium plating like gold.

When used alone or when alloyed with gold and silver, palladium has the same metal properties than other metal jewelry, and it is tarnish free. It also give your consumers a different price point than platinum. Palladium is more precious than silver and is whiter than platinum. Also, its weight is lighter than platinum, so it is preferred for necklaces and bracelets. All these jewelry items contain a more significant amount of gemstones without increasing the overall weight of the jewelry. For this reason, palladium is an excellent choice to make earrings. Due to the increased rise in the price of both gold and platinum, there has been a rise in the use of palladium all over the world.

Palladium is also used to alloy gold in the United States. Making an alloy of palladium and white gold will significantly reduce allergic reactions like dermatitis, skin rashes, and eczema that would have happened due to wearing white gold jewelry made with nickel. In an 18k piece of jewelry, a white gold alloy usually contains 75% gold and 15% palladium. Although there are other metals such as zinc and nickel that have been traditionally used to make white gold, palladium is the best gold alloy for sensitive skin.

Apart from making jewelry, palladium is used in electronics, the chemical industry, auto catalysts, fuel cells and coins. Due to its white appearance, palladium has gained a lot of popularity among men for their wedding bands, also in ladies' engagement and wedding rings.

Tungsten

Tungsten is also referred to as the tungsten carbide. It is a tough, strong, and durable metal. It is also the heaviest metal. Tungsten prides itself in having a unique property; it has a high resistance to scratches. Unlike gold, platinum and titanium, jewelry made from tungsten does not show signs of wear. Technically, you can only scratch tungsten by using materials that are harder than it. These materials include diamonds, sapphires, ceramic and rubies. Tungsten will remain scratch resistant unless you drag the tip of a diamond object along it. Most people want a wedding that is scratch resistant, and it is highly expensive. Tungsten also comes with the following advantages:

- Tungsten has an appealing color to almost all men. Its color is grey-white and is similar to that of white gold or silver.
- Tungsten will always appear new, shiny and bright. It does not need to be polished so that it can be maintained like gold, titanium and platinum jewelry.
- Tungsten is known to withstand wear even when subjected to some of the roughest conditions. This makes it popular among men looking for wedding rings.
- Tungsten can also be inlaid with other metals like gold and platinum, making a perfect looking two-tone combination for wedding rings, especially for men.

However, the range of use for tungsten is more restricted than other metals. Currently, tungsten is mostly used to make men's rings, bracelets and watch lines. Therefore, if you were selling it, your primary target would be men.

Stainless Steel

Stainless steel is a metal that has gained a lot of popularity in recent years. Jewelry made from stainless steel, though not familiar to most people, is a growing niche in the jewelry industry and metal trade. Many people are beginning to know the benefits of stainless steel, with more and more purchases every day. Below are the main advantages of stainless-steel jewelry.

Durable: when it comes to durability, it is true that stainless steel will outlast most metals, including gold and silver. Stainless steel comes naturally as a hard alloy and can withstand a lot of wear and tear. For this reason, a piece of jewelry made from stainless steel will last longer than jewelry made from either gold or silver. This may have led to its increased demand.

Has good material: although gold and silver are both stunning in appearance, they can sometimes get stained very easily after being worn. Jewelry made from this material are easily smudged or stained, so they need to be handled with a lot of care and polished more often to remain new. With stainless steel, you do not need to worry about this. This makes it appealing to many people and raises its demand.

Versatile: stainless steel jewelry is extremely adaptive. It is good to know that different people buy jewelry for various reasons. Some people buy jewelry so that that they feel that they own something valuable, while others will buy jewelry so that they can wear it and look more attractive in public. No matter the reason for you wearing jewelry, you can have a beautiful stainless piece that can fulfill your needs, and this makes stainless steel jewelry more versatile. Trading with stainless steel will therefore mean that you will always have a consistent demand for the product.

Titanium

Titanium is a natural element that has a silver-grayish-white color. Titanium prides itself in being the hardest natural metal ever seen on the earth's surface. It is extremely strong, with three times the strength of steel and many times stronger than gold, silver and platinum, but it is also very lightweight. Pure titanium is also 100% hypo-allergic, so it is safe for any person to wear because it will not cause allergic reactions to the skin.

Image source – Unsplash.com

What are the Advantages of Selling Titanium Jewelry?

At the end of the 20th century, most people have come to see titanium as the best option for jewelry. In the past, most consumers were not aware of the many advantages that this precious metal offers. Apart from its durability and excellent style, it is also affordable and provides health benefits. Below are some of the benefits that come from buying titanium jewelry:

Stronger and More Durable

One of the things that titanium prides itself over other metals is its strength and durability. Unlike gold and silver that scratch easily as a result of daily wear, titanium provides jewelry that is strong and durable even after wearing it for a long time. Titanium can withstand adverse conditions, three times more than what jewelry made from steel can. Titanium is the ultimate choice for people who usually work outdoors or with children that can easily pull the piece of jewelry, leading to damage. Titanium doesn't dent or scratch, nor does it lose its shining properties. It does not corrode nor change its color from wear or passage of time. It is not necessary to polish titanium jewelry because the strength of the metal does not allow any flaws, making the metal very strong and extremely desirable. Additionally, due to its strength, it is used in bolder jewelry designs than other soft metals. Unlike many rings, especially those made from gold that tend to lose its round shape over time, titanium does not lose its form.

Offers Style and Comfort

It is easy to change titanium to fit each person's preference and style. Despite its hardness, titanium can be manufactured in various styles including inlaid metals set with gemstones, or by polishing it in multiple finishes. To have distinctive titanium jewelry, other metal inlays can be added. Metals that can be inlaid to the jewelry include white gold, platinum and yellow gold. This makes room for distinctive patterns for each person. It is also possible to include diamonds or gemstones in titanium jewelry pieces. When diamonds or gemstones are set up together on titanium jewelry, you will have a smooth, clean and stylish look that exceeds a product with gemstones paired with yellow, gold, or silver. You can also polish titanium into a variety of finishes.

Its Availability

Before the 1990s, it was rare to see jewelry made from titanium in the market. However, nowadays, many rings, necklaces, pendants and other jewelry are made from it. As a trader planning to sell jewelry made from titanium, you will not struggle. There is now so much information on how good this product is that so many people want to buy it, either as adventurous shoppers or traditional jewelry lovers. It is no doubt that when more and more people learn about his precious metal, there will be an increased purchase of this product, so any trader will have a broader market.

Titanium is perfectly biocompatible even when in its higher strength alloys called aircraft- grade titanium. Aircraft-grade titanium is more resistant than pure titanium, so it is generally used for dental fittings and surgical implants. Titanium remains the only foreign material that living tissue can be attached to. Individuals who experience allergic reactions after wearing jewelry made from either gold or silver can shift to wearing titanium jewelry without experiencing any skin problems. Unlike gold, silver and other metals that are mixed with other highly allergic substances that cause irritations to the skin, titanium is safe because it is not mixed with such substances. Titanium is at its best when used in its pure form, so it is suitable to a larger number of people.

It is Popular with Men

The rise of the use of titanium in the current world can be attributed to its popularity among men. Many men prefer wearing titanium because it appears more masculine especially due to its sleek and almost space-age look. Men who are not fond of wearing jewelry like to wear watches or rings made from titanium. The durability and strength of titanium is also a major contributing factor to its popularity among men.

Affordability

If you are the kind of trader looking to sell jewelry that almost everybody can afford, then selling titanium jewelry could be the best choice due its low price. Gold, for example, is rated and priced in line with its karat and the intricate preparation process. Many other expensive metals have other kind of metals combined, so they require to be refined before being converted to jewelry. Adding either diamonds or gemstones to this jewelry also increases its cost tremendously.

Contrary to other precious metals, titanium in its natural form can be jewelry without adding any other metal to it; it only needs shaping and styling. Also, due to the short process involved in making it, titanium jewelry's price is lower than other jewelry.

Chapter 3

A Comprehensive Guide to Trading Gold

Gold is a yellow and precious metal with a chemical element of atomic number 79. It is mainly used to make jewelry and decorations as well as guaranteeing the value of currencies. For many years, gold has played a very significant role in the whole world's financial systems. Unlike many other metals available, gold has a value that goes beyond just its usage and application in the industrial world. Although many business sectors including electronics, jewelry and dentistry use gold to make their products, there is no commercial demand to help explain the rise in prices of this precious metal.

Since the early times of civilization, people from all races have viewed gold as a measure of wealth and money. In reality, it remains the misunderstood commodity of the world.

How Much Gold has Been Mined So Far?

There is a limited supply of gold above ground, so finding gold deposits is a tough task. Also, the extraction of this precious metal from gold mines is a costly and time-consuming endeavor. The most exciting thing about the extraction of gold is that it is not only found beneath the ground, but also in oceans. It is estimated that ocean waters have over 20 tons of gold, which is more than the human race has ever mined. However, studies show that a liter of water from the sea has almost 13 billionth of a gram of gold. Did you read that correctly? A billionth!

However, we cannot deny that gold is a rare commodity. According to analysts' estimates, the total supply of gold in the whole world is around 17,000 tons. In fact, if all this gold was used to cover the Center Court at Wimbledon, it would rise only at 9.8 meters from the ground level. Or, if it were melted, it would fit within an Olympics swimming pool and still leave some room unoccupied.

As a trader, you may be asking yourself this question - what really drives the price of gold? Don't worry, as we will now look into this.

What Determines the Price of Gold?

World Gold Council indicates that the annual gold volume has increased three times every year since the early 1970s, whereas the amount of gold sold each year has quadrupled. Since the private ownership of gold became legal in 1972, the price of gold has risen from of $45.75 to its current price today which is $1,307.

There are many factors that usually lead to the rise of the price of gold. They include:

The Supply and Demand of Gold

Just like any other commodity, the cost of gold will be affected by the balance between output and the demand in the market. Usually, when the supply levels of gold fall, the prices will tend to go up, and vice versa. Many factors can lead to a limited supply of gold, including political unrest in countries that are known to produce gold as well as an increase in the mining cost that is often a result of a rise in fuel prices.

Another factor that affects the availability of gold is the price of gold itself. When the price of gold increases, mining becomes a profitable venture, so you expect to find more supply of gold in the market. Similarly, the fall in prices of gold in the market will lead to reduced mining activities, so gold in the market will be limited. Often, demand from related industries, traders, central banks or sovereign wealth funds will affect the prices of gold.

The Economic Data

Economic data, especially in developed countries like the US can impact the prices of gold. Because the US dollar is regarded as the world's reserve currency, having either weak employment or GDP numbers could make the dollar more vulnerable than other currencies. Usually, gold gets the upper hand when the US dollar is weak because it is a competing form of money.

Policies from the Central Bank

Actions and policies made by the Central Bank can significantly affect the price of gold in two ways. First, the Central Bank can decide on whether to contract or grow the supply of money in a given country. These decisions will ultimately drive an increase in the trade of gold because fiat currencies like the US dollar and euro usually compete with gold as a measure and store of value and also as a form of money.

Secondly, central banks are known for holding vast reserves of gold. The decision of the Central Bank to either sell or accumulate more gold reserves can significantly affect the price of gold.

Increased Demand in Instruments that Invest in Gold

Investment organizations like the exchange-traded funds (ETFs) represent a significant segment of gold investment. Most gold ETFs will buy physical gold and keep it for their traders, while some invest in gold futures options or other derivative gold products. Demand for all these products can bring a change in the price of gold.

What are The Top Gold-Producing Countries?

Gold miners extract gold from the ground from all continents except Antarctica. For a long time, South Africa remained a dominant player in the production of gold. However, in the recent past, it has been overtaken by countries like Russia and China. The top ten gold producing countries include:

- China with an annual production of 455 metric tons
- Australia with a yearly output of 270 metric tons
- The United States of America with a yearly output of 209 metric tons
- Canada with a yearly production of 170 metric tons
- Peru with a yearly production of 150 metric tons
- South Africa with an annual output of metric tons of 140 tons
- Mexico with a yearly production of 125 metric tons
- Indonesia with an annual output of 100 metric tons
- Uzbekistan with a yearly production of 100 tons

What Countries Hold the Largest Gold Reserves?

Official reports indicate the figures of gold reserves that were held by each country in 2017. However, it is important to note that the Central Bank does allow independent audits and therefore the real figures may be higher or lower. In the recent past, there are speculations that both China and Russia have large amounts of gold reserves.

- The United States of America has 8,134 tons of gold
- Germany has 3,374 tons of gold

- Italy has 2,452 tons of gold
- France has 2,436 tons of gold
- China has 1,843 tons of gold

The Main Use of Gold

After mining the gold, it is processed by refiners into gold bars that are later sold. The buyers will then transform this gold into items like electronic components, jewelry, and coins. They can also store the gold bars and later sell them as investments.

Just like the supply of gold, the demand for gold in the market is international and revolves around different traders and industries. In recent times, fast-growing economies in the Asian continent such as China and India have radically increased the demand for gold. Four components have led to increased demand for gold. They include:

Jewelry – the jewelry industry uses gold for different commodities like rings, watches, necklaces, pendants, and earrings among many other items. For many years, jewelry makers have had a high demand for gold.

Pirate investors – people and investment funds that need protection against inflation and market crises see gold as a way to preserve their wealth. The demand for gold in the investment sector reveals itself through the sale of gold bars, coins, and funds that trade in the metal.

Technology – due to the ability of gold to conduct electricity and the fact that it does not tarnish, most industries prefer to use gold to make their products. Products such as switches, connectors and relay contacts in cell phones contain gold, and even CPU memory chips and motherboards. Gold is also used with salt to treat arthritis in patients and even in space vehicles to help reflect radiation.

In Central Banks and other Sovereign Wealth Funds – Central Banks and most Sovereign Wealth Funds have gold reserves. Although the major world economy holds a formal gold standard, many countries like France, the United States, Germany, Switzerland, Italy, and China have significant gold reserves as a way to give confidence to their fiat currencies.

Chapter 4

Understanding Gold Trade

Reasons Why You Should Trade Gold

Investors and traders buy gold for many different reasons. The most common ones include the following:

Acts as a hedge against inflammation – gold acts as a perfect hedge against any weakness in the largest world economy, the United States. A vulnerability in the US economy is more likely to be felt by other world economies, and the Central Bank will reiterate by lowering interest rates and increasing the supply of money. If these measures do not spur the demand, there can be significant inflammation and a reduction of purchasing power. Gold, unlike other fiat currencies, will maintain its purchasing power even during times of inflammation.

Gold performs even during global instability – gold prides itself as a commodity that performs even during times of crises. Circumstances such as wars, terrorist attacks or even pandemics usually affect the safety of a metal. Surprisingly, during tough times, gold greatly benefits at the expense of other assets.

There is high speculation on the rise of gold prices – investors who are hopeful about the economic prospects of developing nations like India and China may regard investing in gold as a way to make a fortune. Historically, gold has played a major economic role in these countries, and therefore, more wealth is likely to lead to high demand for gold.

You can use gold to diversify your trading portfolio – most gold traders will use gold to expand and balance their investments. In the past, gold has proved to have a low correlation compared to many classes of assets, making it a more attractive instrument for diversification.

How Gold Investments Works

You should consider investing in gold as a four-tied pyramid, with the safe tier being your foundation and the risk together with potential reward rising as you climb up the pyramid. The pyramid involves the following:

Insurance – gold bullion that you possess

Saving or Investment – this refers to deposited gold bullion, gold certificates, and allocated gold accounts.

Investment – includes gold mining, producing, company shares, and gold ETFs.

Speculation – includes gold CFDs, gold futures, gold explorers' shares, and gold options.

Should You Invest in Gold?

This is not a question that can be answered with a simple yes or no. I shall only lay the foundation by telling you the reasons to invest, and the reasons not to, and this is how you will be able to make an informed decision.

Just like any other investment, when you decide to invest in gold, you will have both profit and losses. The best thing with gold is that in case of calamities or political instability in your area, it may give you the much-needed portfolio for protection. This is the reason that many traders consider investing part of their assets in gold.

Gold gives traders an opportunity to cash in emerging markets with one strength. It is likely that developing economies have suffered long periods of economic and political uncertainties, which means that most citizens may have experienced devaluations in the local currency and might not trust fiat currencies.

As wealth grows in these economies, the demand for gold will also increase. Investors who want to have a share in the growing economies without investing in the local stock and bond markets in these nations might prefer investing in gold.

However, gold trading, just like any other investment, comes with its fair share of risks. When the strength of the dollar rises, or there are fiscal changes from the central banks, the price of gold may fall significantly. If there is a slowdown in either China or India or if gold reserves are sold in large quantities by central banks, this could also lead to a decline in the price of gold.

Finally, if you are considering investing in gold, consider that it is a commodity that is affected by changes in the market. Always invest an amount that will not affect your economic standing, even if it fails.

What Do Experts Say About Gold Trade?

Trade experts have different opinions regarding investing in gold. For example, legendary trader Warren Buffet has a very negative view on gold trading. He bases his argument on the fact that gold does not have earnings and does not pay dividends. Therefore, he argues that it is inferior to stocks. He sees gold as a commodity that has no utility because it is mined from the ground and then stored in a guarded place.

Buffet holds a simple belief when it comes to choosing winning securities. He says that investing is really about picking good stocks at reasonable times and staying with them as far as those companies remain good, and with his philosophy, Buffet invested $ 10,000 in Berkshire Hathaway in 1965 which are worth more than $50 million today. If there is one investment that Buffet will not stash in his portfolio, it is gold, a principle that has prevented him from investing in gold bugs for many years.

However, gold has most of the value components that Buffet would like to see in any of his portfolio holdings. They are the following:

- Gold has protection against economic volatility
- Leverage to gain quick cash liquidity
- Gold gives exposure to high-quality, growth-oriented trade

Famous hedge manager Jim Rogers has always believed that every trader should have physical gold coins as a portfolio to act as a hedge in case other assets collapse.

Manager of Super Hedge Fund George Soros holds positions in gold mining stocks.

How Do You Trade Gold?

There are different ways to trade gold. They include the following:

Gold Bullion

One of the ways to speculate on the price of gold is by holding physical gold bullion like bars or coins. Although this is one of the major ways to invest in gold, investing in bullion requires you to have a secure storage facility. In the end, this storage facility might make holding physical gold expensive.

Some Common Bullion Dealers You Might Consider

JMBullion – an online retailer of precious metal products that was established in 2011. They exclusively deal with physical bullion, selling gold or silver by delivering it directly to your doorstep. JM Bullion's priority is to deliver quality products. They work with mints and distributors directly and inspect all new inventory carefully to ensure that their customers receive high-quality products.

JM Bullion is located in Dallas, TX and it has been fully accredited by the state, the federal government, and distributors alike.

BullionVault – BullionVault allows private investors all over the world to have access to professional bullion markets. In BullionVault, you can buy, sell, and store gold and silver at the lowest costs. It remains the largest online gold investment service that holds over $2 billion for more than seventy thousand users. BullionVault is partly owned by GBIT and Augmentum Capital.

At BullionVault, bars are stored in professional markets in London, Toronto, Zurich, and New York, and you are free to choose where you would like your gold bullion to be stored. Due to their big size, you will definitely benefit from their low-cost storage that also includes insurance.

BullionVault also allows you to sell your bullion any time you want, and they will wire your money the next business day. If you like, you may also withdraw your bars. BullionVault also operates easily and quickly, so you can trade in any quantity of gold within two hours.

APMEX – another leading dealer of precious metals in the United States that understands the needs of gold and silver traders. With more than 15 years in this type of delivery service, APMEX has distinguished itself by giving exceptional customer service, providing quality products and options, as well as brain trust to help traders build their trading portfolio.

APMEX understands that precious metals are not for everyone, so it may not suit traders who like to see wealth purely confined to numbers on pages. They have well-trained personnel to help trades buy and sell precious metals online.

Moneymetals – Moneymetals have state-of-the-art physical security, the lowest fees in the industry, are wholly insured and isolated and have zero shipping costs and insurance.

Gold CFDs

Another way to trade gold is by using CFDs to gain leverage and exposure to various precious metals. A gold CFD is a notional way to buy or sell a given amount of gold and its profit or loss is as per the change in gold prices. Because CFD is derivative, as a trader, you will not have to own gold, but you will still enjoy the benefits as if you owned it. Another great advantage is that its price is lower than gold. The worth of a CFD is measured as the difference in the price of gold at the time it is bought and its current price. This means that the cost of CFD will increase any time there is an increase in gold prices and fall when the prices of gold reduce.

Gold CFDs are one of the most traded, and therefore, it is among the most liquid products a trader can invest in.

CFD investors open an account with a regulated broker and later deposit the funds. The deposited funds will act as a margin against any change in the CFD value.

The good thing is that when investing in CFD, you will not pay for gold storage fees or even roll forward the futures contract every month. As a gold investor, you will not need to worry about the timing and size of the market so that you can benefit from the trade. You will, however, find variations on the availability of gold CFD's depending on how and where you invest. For instance, you may take gold on the quoted price, or you can decide to trade in CFD based on the futures price of the gold. Usually, the standard sizes of the contracts are 10 ounces and 100 ounces. There are also mini contracts a tenth of the standard size.

As said earlier, the value of your CFD will come directly from the change in the value of the amount of gold. The margin, or the money you require to purchase the contract, can be as little as 3% of the total value. You will also incur interest charges, just as if you had borrowed the money to purchase the whole amount. If all the prices go down, and you had a position for a long time, you may receive a margin call, which is an order from the blocker requiring you to submit funds to handle your losses to date.

Let's look at an example to further understand this. Let's say that the price of gold is quoted at $1070 - $ 1070.50. The second price represents the offer price that you would pay. If you were bullish about gold trade and took a mini contract for 10 ounces at the offered rate, it would represent $10,750 value of gold. If the difference were 3%, it would require you to have $322.50 in the account.

After a week, gold may be quoted at $1095 - $1095.50. Closing your contract, you sell at $1095. This will indicate that the value of gold that you have controlled has risen from $10,750 to $10,950 which is $200. Your interest in holding that position for a week will be calculated from this amount and you are likely to get more than 50% of your money in a week.

You should know that CFDs are also high-risk investment instruments and the capital you use is at risk, so there is the need for an experienced investor to acquire the services of a blocker who gives a demo account so that you can know the risks of losing real money in advance.

What Are The Top Gold CFD Brokers?

EToro – eToro was established in 2006, and it provides a platform for online stocks, indices, and commodities in social trading. It was founded by two siblings, Yoni and Rosen, along with their partner David Ring. They founded eToro with the aim to provide a user-friendly online trading financial platform that suits traders with all different levels of trading experience. The business succeeded, and at the moment, it is serving millions of traders worldwide as well as attracting thousands of new users every day. Today, it remains among the premier social trading platforms in the world.

How is eToro Regulated?

EToro is regulated by two separate jurisdictions, Cyprus and the UK.

In the United Kingdom, eToro operates through eToro (UK) LTD and is registered by the UK's Financial Conduct Authority (FCA) under FCA reference number 583263. Both CySEC and FCA operate under the Markets in Financial Instruments Directive (MiFID) which means that eToro is compliant to MiFID broker and thus authorized to operate within the European zone.

In Cyprus, eToro operates under the jurisdiction of the Cyprus Securities Exchange Commission (CySEC). It is licensed under the Cyprus Investment Firm (CIF) with a license number 109/10. It operates under strict regulation requirements. For instance, it operates with adequate capitalization and maintains segregated accounts for the funds of their clients.

Plus500 – Plus500 enables clients to trade popular product CFDs with leverage. Gold and silver are all available on the plus500 trading platform. Plus500 was founded in 2008 and is among the leading online contracts for various (CFDs) platforms to trade in investment instruments like the ETF, Forex, commodities, stocks and market indices. The brand plus500 is both owned and managed by plus500 Ltd which is a listed public company on the main stock exchange market in London. Plus500 was listed in 2013, and its capitalization value has reached over $1 billion in 2014. Currently, plus 500 Ltd operates through many branches carrying the plus500 brand.

FXTM – FXTM was launched in 2011. It is an award-winning online trading platform that gives a safe and secure investing environment covering over 250 instruments across currencies, shares, cryptocurrencies and spot metals. FXTM prides itself to have sponsored Lewis Pugh, UN patron of the oceans to protect the blue waters of the world.

AvaTrade – AvaTrade was initially started in 2006 as AvaFX. It is an online Forex and CFDs broker based in Dublin, Ireland. It specializes in investment services for Bitcoins, equities, Exchange Traded Funds (ETFs), commodities and bonds. Since its establishment, AQvaTrade has widely expanded and serves more than 200,000 accounts globally. It handles over two million transactions monthly and its value exceeds more than $60 million.

FBS – FBS was established in 2009, is based in Belize and is among the leading Forex blockers based in Belize. It is run and managed by a holding company known as FBS Market Inc. Their head office is located at: No 1 Orchid Garden Street, Belmopan, Belize, C.A. FBS provide investors with trading experience by providing educational materials, organizing special events and providing advanced trading technologies. For FBS to handle diverse client requirements, they have different accounts for traders to choose from.

Gold Futures

This is a gold trading derivative that as a trader allows you to see the future prices of gold by purchasing the exchange-traded contracts. Future markets give the traders a liquid and leveraged way to invest. However, you should know that leverage can bring margin calls when the prices reduce. Futures also come with definite expiry dates. This will mean that the trader might either accept the delivery of gold or roll forward the contact to the following month. Generally, trading futures requires active and onerous position maintenance.

Most investors will delay speculating on both ways with the intention of selling what they have bought or purchase back what they have sold before the settling day. They will only need to settle the gains and losses. Through this, they can trade on large amounts, take larger risks, and gain more significant rewards than if they had decided to sell their trades sooner.

How do Gold Futures Compare with Margin?

When you delay a settlement, you create a need for a margin, which is among the most important aspects of buying or selling a gold future.

Margin becomes eminent because when the settlement is delayed, the seller will become nervous because he will be concerned that the fall in the price of gold would drive the buyer away from an already made deal. At the same time, the buyer will become nervous that if the rate of gold rises, the seller might similarly walk away.

Margin resembles the down payment that is usually lodged through an independent central clearer that protects the other party from being tempted to walk away. So, when dealing with gold futures, you will be asked to pay a margin which will depend on the current market conditions. It can be anything between 2 and 20 percent of the total value of what you are dealing with.

When Do You Have To Top Up the Margin?

When you have already bought and the price of gold starts falling, you will be forced to pay more for the margin. As a buyer, you cannot escape paying margin calls when in a falling market unless you sell and that's why investing in futures might cost you more than what you had initially invested.

Gold Leverage

Leverage is the use of different financial instruments or even borrowed capital in increasing possible return on the trade. Traders will leverage their investments with a hope of getting higher profits than what they had borrowed.

Gold ETFs

Although ETFs seem to be the best ways to invest in gold, investors must be aware of the possible risks and costs. A lot of ETFs invest in gold futures or options, which come with some risks. For those EFTs that invest in gold itself, the funds will incur the same storage and security costs that individuals would. At the end, all these costs will be passed on to the investor.

Finally, it is important for you to understand that ETFs are instruments of finance that trade just like stock. When the stock of the market declines, ETFs will not be spared by the same pressure that would drag the stocks down. Some of the leading gold ETFs include:

- iShares Gold Trust
- SPDR Gold Trust
- PowerShares DB Gold Fund
- ETFS Physical Swiss Gold Shares
- Van Eck Merk Gold Trust

5 Top Gold Stocks by Market Capitalization

Investing shares in exploration and mining firms allows investors to make a leveraged bet on the prices of gold. Theoretically, most of the expenses of running a mining company are fixed. This means that when the price of gold increases, the additional revenue will flow at the bottom line as profits. Markets will assign a number for this profit, so bull market investors will make a lot of money by owning these shares.

However, this argument is flawed because the prices of gold will not rise in a vacuum. When the price of gold increases, oil and other products required to run the mining of gold will also rise, so it is a fact that mining shares will rarely outmatch the prices of gold in bull markets.

Barrick – this is the largest gold mining company in the world with its headquarters in Toronto.

Newmont – the history of Newmont in the mining industry dates back to over 95 years. It prides itself as being among the largest gold producers in the world. At Newmont, they believe that they can have a stronger business and add value for all stakeholders.

Newcrest – Newcrest, located in Australia, is among the leading gold mining companies in the world.

Polyus - among the leading gold mining companies with its headquarters in Moscow, Russia.

AngloGold Ashanti – a leading global mining and exploring company based in Johannesburg.

Some Strategies and Tips for Trading Gold

There are countless tips and strategies used by investors to determine the perfect time to either sell or buy gold. Below, we have compiled the three most used tools, tips, and strategies used by investors in conducting gold trade.

Following the Yen – Historically, the Japanese Yen has enjoyed an exceedingly high relationship with the gold price. In fact, charts with gold prices shown in dollars over several timeframes are usually the opposite of the price of USD/JPY in a mirror. The reason for this is because both Yen and gold are perceived as an escape.

Additionally, the price of gold and the Japanese yen are mainly a function of real interest rates and the perception concerning where they are going. Traders seeking to trade in gold want to analyze the Yen to see if it has similar trends.

The Gold/Silver Spread – one of the popular strategies used by long-term investors is the gold/silver spread. For many, many years, gold and silver have been seen as a store of value, although silver has more commercial uses, perhaps due to its lower price.

Some investors will decide to track the ratio and develop pair trading strategies basing their argument on which metal is cheaper than the other. However, just like any other fair trade, it is not guaranteed that historical relationships always remain the same.

Pairing Gold Stocks With Gold – this is another popular way to trade that aims at trading gold stocks as a pair trade against gold. Some investors will track the historical coloration between gold price and stock indexes like the Philadelphia Gold and Silver Sector Index (XAU) or AMEX Gold BUGS (Basket of Unhedged Gold Stocks) Index (HUI)

The reason for this is that gold stocks, especially the companies that do not base their exposure to the metal, leverage ways to buy gold and because both classes of assets should be positively related.

Ways to Leverage Gold Investment

There are several ways to leverage in gold trading and investment. A trader can leverage their experience to gold investment by borrowing from the blocker. Individuals use securities like options and futures contracts that are the bets between market participants where you borrow the principle at bill rates. Using leveraged ETFs and ETNs are another way to carry out this idea.

Additionally, hedge funds can leverage the assets by financing a part of their portfolios with cash proceeds from short sales of other positions.

However, it is important to know that with increased leverage comes greater risk. It can either increase profits or losses. For example, assume you had $5,000 cash in a margin account, you would purchase up to $10,000 worth stock of marginal gold. You are to pay 50 percent of the value of the purchase price whereas your brokerage company will offer the other 50 percent. Now, you will have $10,000 in purchasing power. Leverage will be profitable when your stocks of gold are rising; it will double your profits. However, the effect of multiplying will work the opposite way as well. It will be so especially when the investor chooses to use derivatives like the futures contracts or options to increase the return on value without adding on investment.

Leverage will increase the level of market risk. The downside will not always be limited to the value of the collateral in the gold investment account. Based on the current volatility of a market, your brokerage company might initiate the sale of securities in your account to meet the margin call or can increase the maintenance margin requirements at any moment.

When used wisely and prudently and in the right circumstances, leverage can be a profitable tool. Both futures contracts and other derivatives give considerable flexibility in different leverage, as investors are not obliged to take advantage of the maximum allowed. Also, it is important for investors to generate the above average returns by exercising so much leverage that it would expose them to excessive risk. As a trader, it is advisable to consult with a trading advisor in order to choose the best investment vehicles that offer high-quality liquidity and leverage.

How to Invest In Gold as a Beginner

As we have seen before, there are many ways to trade in gold, and for those of you who are just beginning, you need to do some background work.

Bullion

The most obvious way to own gold is by buying physical bars and coins. The trickiest part for beginners is finding a dependable bullion dealer.

Image source – Pixabay.com

References – it is good to ask clients about their buying experience.

Reputation – when doing business with any bullion firm, make sure to check its track record. This information is readily available online. Look at the feedbacks given by clients on each bullion before deciding to start dealing with them.

Price Comparison – a dealer with a good reputation will charge a fair price for both coins and bars, and the prices will vary for each item. However, making a bit of comparison on prices will help you pay a fair price. Always note that the price of physical gold can differ from futures and ETFs.

ETFs - the best thing about investing in ETFs is the amount of fees charged to the client. The funds will incur costs like the bullion storage costs in case of physical gold or the trading costs in case of ETFs that trade in gold futures. The costs are forwarded to the ETF buyers and are part of the management fees.

Sites like the ETF database have a wealth of information on the funds that include the costs. When evaluating the funds, ensure you compare apple-to-apple. This means that you should compare the funds with other funds according to the purchasing method.

Equities

The equities for precious metals are not only affected by the gold price but also by the stock market vagaries. However, as a trader, you can protect yourself by investing in companies that have successful track records and highly experienced management teams. You can start your search from the company's annual report as well as with reports from analysts.

CFD'S

If you are a beginner thinking about buying gold through CFDs, you should first make sure that you have a regulated and reputable broker to work with. You should also thoroughly investigate the fees applied by the broker so that you can compare them with other brokers.

Some of the Basics of Trading Gold

Below are some tips that traders can keep in mind when investing in gold. However, you should not take this as investment advice. As a trader, you must determine on your own what is best for your specific situation.

The Size of Purchase – a good reason to hold gold is that it acts as a haven or insurance for your portfolio. Therefore, you should consider the kind of exposure you wish to have. As a new metal trader, you might be carried away and have a long position in metal.

The Physical Gold – some traders might decide to avoid physical gold because they can easily gain exposure through either stocks or ETFs. However, if holding physical gold would act as an insurance against financial debacle, then it is advisable to have a part of your investment in it.

The Position of the Dollar – having a lot of information about the dollar is the most important thing new traders should focus on, as well as the factors that move the current market. All these factors might have a very significant effect on the prices of gold.

Being a contrarian – just like any other precious asset, the price of gold is sometimes subject to a herd mentality. When there are bad sentiments about gold that is the best moment to buy. Likewise, when the markets represent a bullish environment, it is also the best time to sell your gold. You can use different ways to gauge sentiments, including reports of traders commitment published by CFTC.

Long–term Observation – gold is known to be a volatile asset that can have many price swings. Additionally, gold has a very long trade history. As a trader, you may need to look at key long-term support and levels of resistance to get clues on where this metal may be heading next.

Chapter 5

What Traders Need To Know About Silver

Silver is a shiny metal that has several extraordinary properties. Its properties include malleability, flexibility, as well as being beautiful and lustrous. Silver also allows the reflection and conduction of electricity. It can also kill bacteria. Silver has many properties, making it a precious metal in different categories of industries including electronics, jewelry, medicine, and energy. All these properties reveal why silver is extremely important to the global economy.

Silver is a rare metal, and together with gold and six other platinums is in a group known as precious metals. For a very long time, people have viewed silver as an investment and store of value.

When Did Mining of Silver Begin?

The mining of silver began in Asia during the time of ancient civilization, over five thousand years ago. Around 1,800 years later, the Greek Empire started mining silver to be used as currency, and during the rule of the Roman Empire, silver was an essential trading commodity in the Asian spice routes.

The turning point of the commodity came when the Spanish conquered the New World in the 15th century. There was a dramatic increase in the mining of silver in Peru, Bolivia and Mexico between 1500 and 1800 AD. These countries recorded 85% of the total production of silver in the world as the Spanish gained popularity in America.

Since then, there have been discoveries in the USA, Central America, Europe, and Australia and this has led to increased global production.

The Amount of Silver That Been Mined Until Today

Even though silver has been mined for a long time, the production and reserves of silver are limited.

A report from the US Geological Survey in 2004 estimated the total silver mined to be 1.26 million metric ton – with about half of it being mined in the last sixty years. Other recent estimates say that the total silver mined is 1.5 million metric tons, which is only equivalent to a 52-meter cube of silver.

Where is Silver Found?

It is rare to find silver naturally in the earth's crust. Instead, it is found as a byproduct when miners are extracting gold, lead, zinc or copper. In recent years, the production of silver has declined due to a drop in lead, gold, and zinc.

The Top Ten Producers of Silver in the World

- Mexico – 186.2 million ounces annually
- Peru – 147.7 million ounces annually
- China – 112.4 million ounce annually
- Chile – 48.1 million ounces annually
- Russia – 46.6 million ounces annually
- Australia – 43.6 million ounces annually
- Bolivia – 43.5 million ounces annually
- Poland – 38.5 million ounces annually

- United States of America – 35.4 million ounces annually
- Argentina – 30.0 million ounces annually

Countries with the Largest Reserves of Silver:

Silver reserves refer to the amount of economically minable silver available in the ground. Mining it is expensive, and the price of the metal will determine whether it is worth carrying mining.

Top 5 Countries with the Largest Silver Reserves

- Peru – 120 Metric tons
- Australia – 89 Metric Tons
- Poland- 85 Metric Tons
- Chile – 77 Metric Tons
- China – 39 Metric Tons

Three Main Uses of Silver

In jewelry: silver prides itself as lustrous, beautiful, and workable. This makes it a popular choice for earrings, necklaces, rings, and bracelets. Most manufacturers prefer to use sterling silver, which is 92.5% pure silver and 7.5% copper.

In technology: silver serves a variety of purposes in technology. They include:

In electronics- Silver has excellent electric conductivity, making it the best choice for the production of switches, printed circuit boards, and V screens.

Image Source – Unsplash.com

Solar – when silver is ground into a powder, it can be used to produce solar cells.

Brazing/Soldering – silver plays a major role in the strengthening of connections of pipes, faucets, ducts and electrical wires.

Ball Bearings – silver electroplating plays a major role in strengthening ball bearings.

Medicine – silver acts as a biocide and also kills harmful germs.

Catalysts – catalysts enhance chemical processes. The unique properties of silver make it an ideal catalyst commodity for the production of ethylene oxide and formaldehyde.

Private Investors: persons and investment funds buy silver so that they can protect their portfolios against losses that might come from inflation or crises in the market. Traders buy silver bars, coins, and funds that trade in metal.

What Determines the Price of Silver?

As it is a volatile commodity, silver reacts to industrial and economic data. The following factors are the major drivers of the price of silver:

Supply and Demand

There is a solid relationship between the demand and supply of silver and its price. Silver is a limited commodity and in the recent past, its production has declined. According to experts, the decline is bound to continue due to silver's increased mining costs. Again, the demand for silver, remains stable, with 50% coming from the industry.

As a trader, you need to pay a lot of attention to occurrences that affect the demand/supply equilibrium.

From another perspective, any change in investors' appetite for silver, which is more volatile than demand, might also drive prices.

Demand in Industries

The demand for silver by different industries can have a major impact on the price of silver. The photography industry is no longer in need of silver as it used to. The use of stainless steel has taken the place of silver to make items like the flatware, and a lot of mirrors today contain aluminum instead of silver.

However, industries such water purification and solar will continue to use silver due to its unique and physical characteristics.

Inflation and the State of US Dollar

Investing in silver is among ways that an investor can protect himself from losing purchasing power as a result of inflation and the weak US dollar.

Commodities like silver are usually priced in US dollar and have a strong inverse relationship with the dollar. This means that when the dollar becomes weak, silver prices tend to rise. Individuals buying silver using another type of currency enjoy more purchasing power when the dollar is weak and less purchasing power when the dollar is strong.

Most people view silver as an alternative currency, just like gold or platinum. When a currency loses value or inflation strikes, most investors will turn to silver as a reliable store of value.

Scrap Metals from Silver

Silver scrap metal plays a large role in determining the supply of silver available in the market, thereby affecting its price. In the past, the main source of scrap metal was from the photography industry. However, today, due to the popularity of digital photography, silver is not largely used in the industry. Scrap traders recycle large volumes of photographic film to use for silver content.

The rise in the price of silver would lead to an increased supply of scrap to the market which in turn can lead to reduced prices of silver.

Prices of Gold

For a long time, the prices of gold and silver have had a very close relationship. Most investors will use the price ratio of gold and silver and base their decision to buy either of the commodity in their ratio movements.

Chapter 6

How to Trade Silver

Before engaging in silver trade, you must know that just like any other investment, investing in silver has both potential risks and rewards. However, investing in silver as a way of diversifying your assets could have many benefits.

Reasons that Might Make You Invest in Silver

Traders will invest in silver for different reasons. The most common reasons for trading in silver include:

You Can Use Silver to Mitigate Risk

One of the main reason that traders invest in silver is to give protection in case of economic crises.

Generally, when there is a crisis, central banks will react by lowering interest rates and increasing the supply of money. This might weaken the currency and remove confidence in stock and bond markets. Unlike financial commodities that can be created on paper, silver is a physical asset and thus cannot be created on paper. There is little supply of silver above ground, so it is more likely to hold its value during a time of crisis than financial assets.

Be Able to Bet on the Industrial Strength in the World Economy

Silver is an important commodity in many industries and if the global economy was a strong economy, it would reflect in a rise in the price of silver. For example, the demand for silver is very high in India, so when these and other upcoming markets grow, their demand for silver also increases tremendously.

You Can Speculate When the Supply of Silver is Diminishing

One of the most appealing reasons to trade in silver is its supply picture. In the recent past, the decreased price of silver and expensive mining costs have led to a fall in its production. If the prices do not rise substantially, a lot of silver mining projects will remain inactive. Additionally, if the supply for scrap metal as well as the cost of mining remains low, prices of silver would rise.

Investment Demand for Silver Might Increase

Although industrial demand for silver remains consistent, investment demand can come with advantages. When there is an increase in the investment demand, the prices of silver are more likely to increase too, especially if supply remains the same.

A good reason that demand investment might rise is due to the gold/silver ratio which approaches its highest level in 10 years. Because gold is more expensive than silver, most investors might consider buying silver because they believe that the rate might be lower in the future.

How Do You Invest in Silver?

Traders have different ways to invest in silver:

Silver Bullion

The most direct way to invest in silver is with physical silver bullion like bars and coins. However, for you to invest in silver bullion, you must have a safe storage facility. Ultimately, the cost of storage and the low value-to-weight ratio could mean that holding physical silver may not to be the best idea.

Silver Futures

COMEX division of the Chicago Mercantile Exchange (CME) gives a contract on silver that will settle into 5,000 troy ounces.

The contracts will trade globally on the CME Globex electronic trading platform and have expiration months.

Traders will use futures as derivative instruments to make leveraged bets on the prices of commodities. In case there is a decline in prices, investors will be forced to add their margin deposit so that they can maintain their positions. When they expire, the contracts are physically settled by delivering silver.

When investing in silver futures, you must put in place a high-level of sophistication because some factors like storage costs and interest rates can affect the prices.

What are Silver Options on Futures?

There are options available for derivative instruments that use leverage to trade in commodities, and just like futures, they have an expiry date. However, options may have a strike price, which refers to the price above which the option will finish in the money.

When purchasing contracts, the buyers of options will pay the price referred to as a premium. An option bet will only succeed if the future silver price rises above the strike price by a greater amount than the premium paid for the contract. Therefore, for option traders to benefit from their investment, they must make the right bet on the size and timing of the move in silver futures.

Silver ETFs

ETFs are instruments of finance that will trade just like shares on the exchange, the same way that stocks do. Although investing in ETFs seem to be the perfect way of investing in silver, investors should know the cost and risks involved.

Most ETFs will invest in silver futures or options. For ETFs that invest in physical silver, the funds will be storage and security costs, just like for individuals. At the end, all these costs will be placed on the trader.

When there is a decline in stock markets, the price of ETF will sometimes decline as well. Investors will view their silver investment act the same as a stock exchange.

Four Leading Silver ETFs

- ETFS Physical Silver Shares
- iShares Silver Trust
- E-TRACS UBS Bloomberg CMCI Silver ETN
- PowerShares DB Silver Fund

Shares Trading in Silver Mining Companies

Theoretically, buying shares in silver mining companies will help investors have a leveraged bet on silver prices.

- Many costs of operating a mining company may almost be fixed
- As the price of silver rises, additional revenues ought to reflect at the bottom line as profits.
- A multiple will be assigned to these profits, so bull market traders ought to make more revenue when they own shares.

However, the price of silver cannot rise in a vacuum.

When there is a rise in the price of silver, there will usually be a rise in the cost of mining as well. It is rare for mining shares to outdo the price of silver during bull markets.

Wheaton Precious Metals: a Canadian gold and silver mining company. It is also a streaming company.

Pan American silver: this is also a Canadian company that is involved in exploration, extraction, processing and refining silver from the mines.

Silver Standard: a Canadian company that engages in acquiring, exploring, developing and operating properties of precious metals in the Americas.

CFDs

Another way to invest in silver is by using the contract for difference (CFD) derivative instrument. CFDs will help investors to speculate on silver prices. You will know the value of a CFD by finding the difference between silver price during the purchasing time and its current price.

Most brokers regulated globally give CFDs on silver. A client will deposit funds with the brokers that will serve as a margin. The good thing in trading CFDs is that it allows traders to have an exposure to prices of silver without necessarily purchasing shares, ETFs, futures or even options.

Chapter 7

Comprehensive Guide to Platinum Trading

Platinum is part of six metals called platinum group metals (PGMs), and it is mainly used to make jewelry and car converters. Traders will buy platinum for the same reasons they would buy silver and gold.

Why is Platinum Valuable

Platinum is a chemical compound rarely found in the earth's crust. It is a greyish-white commodity and one of the most intriguing metal commodities due to its user base that defies simple categorization. Business environments like the automotive industry have a high demand for platinum to be used in catalytic converters, while investors will see this metal as a financial asset and a store of value. Jewelry traders like platinum because of its beautiful and shiny appearance and its tarnishing resistance.

Is Platinum a Rare Commodity?

When you consider the use of platinum and compare it to gold, they may look the same. However, platinum may even be rarer than gold. Miners extract about 130 million tons of platinum compared to over 1,700 million tons of gold.

The mining and extraction of platinum are also more consuming than the mining of gold. The process of extracting platinum from its ore can take over six months and may need ten tons of ore to have one ounce of platinum. The cost of mining one ounce of platinum is almost two times that of mining one ounce of gold. There are only two hundred million ounces of platinum available above the ground compared to five billion ounces of gold.

Where Platinum Comes From

Platinum is a dense, malleable and ductile metal. Platinum is extracted from ore bodies in mines that have platinum group elements (PGMs). These elements include platinum, osmium, palladium, iridium, ruthenium, and rhodium. All these elements have the same chemical, anatomical, and physical characteristics.

Platinum is generally extracted by miners from placer deposits that occur naturally as concentrations of heavy metal. These deposits will accumulate due to gravity effects on the moving particles. Miners can also extract platinum from Sperrylite and cooperate, that are also ores containing platinum.

Scrap metal recycling will also give a part of the annual supply of metal.

The amount of platinum mined in a year is over 170,000 kilograms. However, this amount has reduced in recent years because companies have cut on production and others have even closed the mines as a result of low prices.

The Bushveld Complex Company in South Africa has the largest platinum reserves and supplies with over 75% of the world's output.

What are the Top Five Platinum Mining Countries?

1. South Africa: 120,000 kilograms
2. Russia: 23,000 kilograms
3. Zimbabwe: 13,000 kilograms
4. Canada: 9,000 kilograms

5. United States of America: 3,900 kilograms

Platinum is demanded in all the corners of the world. Europe, for instance, accounts for almost half of the total annual demand for platinum, whereas both Japan and North America account for between 10% and 15% each. China accounts for almost 5% of the total yearly demand for the metal, and the remaining 20% is shared among the rest of the world. The gross demand for platinum also includes the amount of platinum recycled.

Countries with the Largest Reserves of PGM

PGM reserves refer to the amount of economically mineable metals available in the ground. South Africa enjoys over 90% of the world's PGM reserves.

However, as mentioned earlier, mining is an expensive activity and therefore, metal prices determine whether it is economical to mine it or not.

What Are the Top Five PGM Reserves?

1. South Africa: 63,000,000 kilograms
2. Zimbabwe: 1,200,000 kilograms
3. Russia: 1,100,000 kilograms
4. USA: 900,000 kilograms
5. Canada: 310,000 kilograms

In the 1970s, major applications for platinum were developed when air quality ordered catalytic converters to be used in the production of automobiles.

Top Platinum Uses

In Automobile Industry: the automobile industry consists of 40% of the total demand for platinum. Automobile manufacturers will use platinum in catalytic converters to control harmful exhaust emissions.

Image source – Unsplash.com

Jewelry: The jewelry industry uses more than 30% of the total global demand for platinum. Its shiny appearance and its resistance to tarnishing make it ideal for a variety of rings, bracelets, necklaces, and watches.

Industrial Uses: The use of platinum in the industries accounts for more than 25% of its total demand. Products such as oxygen sensors, spark plugs, turbine engines, anti-tumor agents, dentistry and dental crowns, and measure magnets all contain platinum.

Investment Demand: Investors accounts for more than 5% of the total global demand for platinum in a year. Countries such as the United States, Australia, Canada, China and Isle of Man all mint platinum coins for traders. Traders can also buy platinum bullion in for of bars and ingots

What Affects the Prices of Platinum?

The demand and supply of platinum have an abnormal equation. Historically, the demand for platinum comes from both the investors and the industry, making it similar silver and gold but different from all other metals.

South Africa is the largest supplier of platinum in the world and therefore, you cannot ignore the impact that this nation has on its price. Below are some significant determinants of platinum prices:

The Economy of South Africa

Apart from accounting for over 75% of the world annual output of platinum, South Africa accounts for over 95% of proven platinum reserves globally.

As it is a developing nation, the markets in South Africa are volatile and not predictable. Events such as labor strikes and political instability can slow down the production of platinum. Additionally, economic occurrences and the way politicians and leaders respond to these events can greatly impact the supply of platinum in the market. Government taxation, nationalization of assets, as well as the restriction of land use all have the potential to affect the amount of mine produced.

Global Auto Industry Health

Catalytic converters utilize more than 40% of the total supply of platinum. Without a doubt, trends in the auto sector have a lot of impact on the price of platinum. Usually, the price of platinum will be much higher when the auto industry is doing well but will slump when the auto industry is unhealthy.

Trends in environmental laws can have far-reaching effects on the prices of platinum. When developing countries are passing stricter laws and vehicles emission standards, the price for platinum responds positively. Generally, the health of the auto industry reflects the state of the overall economy, and therefore strong economic growth will bond well for prices of platinum.

Development of Electric Vehicles

The progressive development of electric vehicles and their demand could result in a decline in the demand for platinum. Several factors such as oil prices and the implementation of stricter air quality laws could be the reason for the rise in demand of electric vehicles.

Catalytic Converter Technology Changes

Advancements in technology, such as how auto industries reduce the exhaust emissions could affect the demand for platinum.

The relatively high prices of platinum may cause automakers to seek other technologies. Palladium easily replaces a part of platinum used in catalytic converters. If these improvements in technology continue, the demand for this metal is likely to further reduce. Eventually, the changes happen quickly due to the high price of this metal.

Investment Demand

Investment demand represents a small portion of the gross annual demand. However, when the strength of the dollar is low and the cost of gold is high, many individuals might consider substituting dollar investments to platinum.

Main Reasons to Invest in Platinum

Investing in platinum gives a way to have a bullish view on worldwide growth. Additionally, most investors will view platinum as a store of value and as an insurance policy against weakness in the dollar. Below, we will give you the three major reasons for investing in platinum:

You Will Be Able to Bet on Industrial Growth

The auto industry is among many industries that use platinum to make its products. Almost one in every five products manufactured uses platinum in one way or another before being transformed into its final state.

As emerging markets grow, the demand for manufactured products will also grow. Therefore, investing in platinum is a way to bet on the growth of the global industry.

Platinum Investment is a Hedge on Weak US dollar

Platinum is the same as many other products in the sense that it moves inversely in relation to the US dollar. This makes investing in platinum a way to benefit from a weak US dollar.

Uncontrolled spending by the government of the United States has led to large debts and deficits in the world's largest economy. The government of America does not have the potential to print enough dollars to clear the debt which can result in weakened purchasing power. Therefore, investing in platinum together with other hard assets will protect investors from wealth erosion that could result from having a weak US dollar.

You Can Use Platinum to Speculate on Demand/ Supply Imbalance

The supply for platinum is limited and is largely concentrated in only a few countries. In the recent past, many companies have shut down their mines or reduced the production of platinum in response to low prices. As mentioned earlier, there are a couple of reasons for the rise in the price of platinum. They include:

- Strike of workers in mining sites, especially in South Africa

- Failure of safety measure in mines

- Increase in consumer demand in developing countries

• Stricter exhaust emission standards

As it is an already constrained industry, the imbalance could highly increase the price of platinum.

What Risks Come With Investing in Platinum?

Just like investing in any other commodity, investing in platinum does have its fair share of risks. These include:

- Retarded growth in the auto industry or even a global recession would lead to a reduction in prices.
- Development of new technology for automotive emissions would cause the prices to lower.
- When the US dollar is strong, the prices of platinum are bound to fall significantly.

How Do Experts View Platinum Investing?

Some experts view platinum trading as an alternative trading commodity to gold. For instance, Head of Real Asset Strategy at Well Fargo John LaForge thinks that the prices of platinum represent a more affordable way to trade in precious metals than gold.

Simona Gamborini, another leading expert, believes that long term fundamentals that include the use of platinum in applications in industries and constrained supplies to be the reasons for bullishness: she says that auto sales in Europe have grown stronger with time and till now, there are no signs that political uncertainty will have a big impact on the consumption of the metal. Again, a lack of adequate investment and depletion of reserves in South Africa could continue to constrain the growth output.

SP Angel, another expert, is pessimistic about platinum trade and believes that an increase in palladium used as catalytic converters has curtailed the demand for platinum.

How Do You Invest in Platinum?

There are many ways to invest in this precious commodity. They include the following:

Platinum Bullion

Traders can purchase platinum bullion bars and coins from metal dealers just as you would buy silver or gold bullion. In the USA, for instance, investors can buy American Platinum Eagle Coins with a purity of 99.95%

Platinum bars are invented at foundries in various sizes such as one ounce, ten ounces, and one kilogram. When you buy physical platinum, you will need storage facilities like safety deposit boxes or secure safes.

Below are some online platinum bullion dealers that you can trade with:

- BullionVault
- JMBullion
- APMEX
- Moneymetals

Platinum future

New York Mercantile Exchange (NYMX), part of the Chicago Mercantile Exchange, gives platinum futures contracts. These derivative commodities have a long history among other metal products invested in the exchange.

Traders trading in futures will leverage to purchase contracts according to platinum prices. If there is a decline in platinum prices, investors will have to add additional margin so that they can maintain their positions. Traders will either roll their future contracts forward every month or accept physical delivery. As a trader investing in the futures market, you should remain sophisticated and ensure you actively maintain positions.

Option buyers can pay the price called a premium to buy contacts. An option call bet will only succeed when the future price of platinum rises above the strike price by a figure more than what was paid for the contract. Therefore, individuals trading in options will have to be right about both the size and timing of the move in platinum future so that they can benefit from their trade.

Platinum Options

Platinum options are a type of derivative instrument that trades on NYMEX. Just like futures, options have an expiration date. The difference between them is that options will succeed if the price amounts to the strike price by the expiration date. Options traders will pay a premium to the seller to get the right to exercise the option in the future. Investors in options should have correct determinations concerning the size and the timing of the move of platinum so that they can benefit from their trade.

Platinum ETFs

Platinum ETFs are financial instruments that trade as shares in the same way that stock does. You can trade in platinum with the use of the following Exchange-Traded funds (ETFs).

- iPath Dow Jones - UBS Platinum ETN
- ETFS Physical Platinum Shares
- Sprott Physical Platinum and Palladium Trust

- Shares in Mining Companies

Many companies traded by the public have exposure to the prices of platinum.

Although trading in companies can bring a leveraged way to have exposure to the prices of platinum, many of these companies will also have a large exposure to other precious metals. Additionally, factors including company management and the overall stock market might also impact these investments:

Anglo Platinum: Anglo Platinum is the largest platinum producer in the world. It was founded in 1995 and has over 28,000 employees. Anglo Platinum accounts for over 38% of the total platinum supply.

Impala Platinum: Impala Platinum is among the leading producers of platinum in the world. It was founded in 1967 and has over 53,000 employees. It was originally called Bishops Platinum.

Lonmin: Lonmin is a British producer of platinum. It was founded in 1909 and has over 24,000 employees. Lonmin once owned the British newspaper.

Norilsk Nickel: Norilsk Nickel is a Russian platinum and nickel mining and smelting company. It was founded in 1993 and has more than 96,000 employees.

Sibanye Stillwater: Founded in 2012, it is the largest producer of platinum in the world. It also prides itself in being among the top ten producers of gold in the world.

Platinum CFDs

Another way to invest in platinum is through the use of a contract for difference (CFD) derivative instrument. CFDs will allow investors to speculate on platinum prices without buying bullion, ETFs, futures, options, or even mining shares.

You find the value of CFD by getting the difference between the prices of platinum during the time of purchase and its current price. When there is an increase in the prices of platinum, the value of CFD will increase, whereas in the case of a decline in platinum prices, the value of the CFD will decrease.

Most of the regulated blockers globally give platinum CFDs. Clients will deposit funds with the broker to serve as a margin. The advantage of trading in CFD is that investors will have exposure to platinum without necessarily buying or even storing bullion, or managing complex futures or options positions.

Chapter 8

The Ultimate Guide to Palladium Trading

Palladium belongs to PGM groups and is used to make catalytic converters, dental equipment, and electronic parts.

Why is Palladium Valuable?

Palladium is a lustrous, silver-like whitish metal commodity. It forms the platinum group of metals together with osmium, iridium, rhodium, platinum, and ruthenium.

PGM are scarce commodities. According to a survey, the PGM group of metals makes about 0.0005 parts per one million of the earth's crust. PGMs are also superior catalysts that allow chemical reactions to happen more quickly.

William Hyde Wollaston, an English chemist, discovered palladium in 1803 by mixing platinum with nitric acid and hydrochloric acid and found that an element was formed. This shiny and malleable element later became a prevalent metal used in the jewelry industry.

However, the luxurious use for this metal was converted to essential use after the advent of modern emission standards for automobiles.

Since 1989, palladium has been used mainly in catalytic converters in the automobile industry. Currently, more than 75% of the total 208,000 kilograms of palladium mined per year is used in the automobile industry.

Main Characteristics of Palladium

Palladium has the lowest melting point and density of all PGM metals. However, just like any other metal in this group, palladium is a noble metal that does not corrode or rust due to oxygen. Additionally, acid cannot corrode or penetrate the metal to damage it.

All these characteristics together with its shiny, lustrous look make palladium an ideal commodity for making jewelry. However, its lower density makes it less desirable than platinum to make high-end jewelry products.

One of the unique characteristics of palladium is its unusual ability to absorb hydrogen. In fact, palladium absorbs a hydrogen volume equal to 900 times its volume. This characteristic makes this element the preferred choice for fuel cells and the nuclear industry.

The Evolvement of Palladium Industry

Although palladium was discovered as early as the 19th century, at the time, there were no viable commercial uses for this metal, as this started in the 20th century.

Palladium was first used in the photography industry. However, because the metal was rare and expensive, it was not widely used. During the 1920s and 1930s, there were new discoveries of metal deposits in South Africa, and later in Canada. Soon afterward, the dental industry started to use palladium and platinum to make alloys for crowns and bridges.

During the 1960s, after new research in the catalytic characteristics of palladium, the metal started being used in the production of polyester and cracking fuel. With the implementation of more strict automobile emission standards in the 1970s, the demand for this metal increased significantly. The fact that it is able to absorb carbon monoxide made it the most appropriate metal to design catalytic converters.

What Drives Palladium Prices?

Only a handful of countries have a concentrated supply of palladium, and the overwhelming demand comes from the automotive industry. All these factors make palladium an extremely volatile commodity.

Below are six significant drivers of palladium prices:

Demand in Vehicles

Almost three-quarters of all palladium produced is used in catalytic converters in the automobile industry. For this reason, demand for vehicles will play an important role in determining its price. Cars that use diesel will use platinum to make catalytic converters, while those that use gasoline fuel will use palladium. Therefore, the demand for vehicles for countries that use gasoline fuel like China and the USA will lead to a higher demand for palladium than countries like Europe that use diesel vehicles more.

China alone accounts for more than a third of the global palladium demand.

Supply from South Africa and Russia

South Africa and Russia account to over 75% of the combined supply of palladium in the world. Therefore, changes in supply from these two countries can greatly affect the prices of palladium.

Nornickel, a Russian company, remains the world's largest supply of palladium. Several factors could affect the supply of palladium from Russia, including a change in mining regulations, political sanctions, and export restrictions.

South Africa supplies almost the same amount of palladium as Russia. Interruptions in electricity supply, high costs of fuel, and high construction costs have led to the disrupted supply of palladium in the past.

Demand in Investment

Palladium, just like any other precious metal, has gained a lot of interest from many investors. Investors can either buy ETFs, bullion and other financial products to enable them to gain exposure to this metal. The palladium market has a history of having thin liquidity and large price swings. When traders either exit or enter this market, investors might experience large price swings.

Prices of Palladium-like Commodities

Various PGM metals can serve the same purpose as that of palladium, especially in the automotive industry. When there is a change in the price of these commodities, it is going to affect the demand for palladium. For example, rhodium and platinum can both be used in catalytic converters. If the price of this metal is less than the price of palladium, most manufacturers would prefer to use those commodities rather than using palladium.

Looking at it from a different perspective, when the prices of palladium reduce compared to the price of platinum and rhodium, most manufacturers will increase the demand for the commodity. Diesel catalytic converters use approximately between 25% and 50% of the world's supply of palladium. If the price of palladium decreases, new demand will arise from the diesel sector.

US Dollar and Inflation

Trading in palladium is the way that investors can protect themselves from losing purchasing power due to inflation and a weakened dollar. Palladium is usually priced in US dollars and it exhibits a strong inverse relationship with the US dollar. This means that when the dollar becomes weak, palladium prices tend to rise. Traders who will buy palladium using any other currency will enjoy more purchasing power when the dollar is weak and on the side have low purchasing power when the US dollar becomes strong.

Palladium is a precious metal that is seen as an investment. During times of currency devaluation and inflation, investors usually turned to precious metals as a dependable store of value.

Recycling

The amount of palladium recycled can have an enormous impact on the prices of palladium. A lot of recycling is done from the catalytic converters in the auto industry. However, there is a drop in the value of palladium in automobiles in comparison to the value of steel. This means that higher prices of steel could lead to increased vehicle recycling which would result in great amounts of palladium being recycled. Having large amounts of recycled palladium means that the prices of palladium metal will be low.

How Does the Production of Palladium Happen?

Mining

Palladium is mined as an ore body containing other PGM metals. Miners will generally extract PGM mineral deposits that occur naturally in concentrations of heavy minerals. These deposits will accumulate due to the effects of gravity on moving substances. The deposits are found in rocks like chromite, norite, and dunite.

Palladium is produced as a by-product when other metals are being produced. For instance, both the Russian Norilsk and Canadian Sudbury miners extract palladium and other platinum group metals as a by-product of copper and nickel.

However, the case is different in South Africa where the Bushveld complex contains large deposits of PGM metals and therefore, mining them on their own is economically justifiable. This region has over 90% of the world's proven PGM metal reserves.

Processing

When palladium and other PGMs are extracted, processing is done with the use of froth flotation techniques. Machines are used to crush the rocks and these rocks are placed in tanks containing chemicals. This helps in separating valuable PGM metals from clay and any invaluable rocks.

Recycling

Scrap metal recycling will provide a part of the yearly production of palladium. Surveys estimate the amount of palladium, rhodium, and platinum recovered by recyclers to be around 125,000 kilograms in a year. This also includes 56,000 kilograms from catalytic converters for the automobile industry.

What is the Availability of Palladium?

The fraction in the mass of metal available in the earth's crust is the accurate barometer to show how rare metal is. By using this measure, all PGM metals apart from platinum and osmium are seen as an extremely rare commodity. Platinum and osmium are available at 5 and 1.5 parts per billion of the earth's crust, respectively. All other PGMs are available in less than one part per billion of the earth's crust.

What are the Top Five Palladium Producing Countries?

Russia: 82,000 kilograms annually

South Africa: 73,000 kilograms annually

Canada: 23,000 kilograms annually

United States: 13,200 kilograms annually

Zimbabwe: 10, 000 kilograms annually

Countries with the Largest PGM Reserves

PGM reserves refer to the amount of economically minable metals available in the ground. South Africa has the largest amount of PGM reserves globally which consists of 90% of the total earth's PGM. However, as mentioned earlier, mining is an expensive activity and the price of the metal will ultimately determine whether it is economically viable to mine the metal.

- South Africa: 63,000,000 kilograms
- Zimbabwe: 1,200,000 kilograms
- Russia: 1,100,000 kilograms
- United States: 900,000 kilograms
- Canada: 310,000 kilograms

In the 1970s, when air quality laws demanded catalytic converters to be used in automobiles, the demand for palladium rose considerably. However, other sectors are also dependent on the supply of this rare commodity.

What are the Top Uses of Palladium?

Catalytic Converters: palladium prides itself in having unusual chemical characteristics making it ideal to produce catalytic converters, as it can trap carbon monoxide in order to reduce pollution.

In Electronics: Multi-layer ceramic capacitors (MLCC) allow to control the flow of current in circuits. Palladium or silver and palladium alloy are mainly used to make MLCCs. Palladium is also used to make plating materials and hybrid integrated circuits.

Dental Sector: alloys of palladium with any of the following metals; gold, silver, copper or zinc are used to make dental inlays, crowns, and bridges.

Miscellaneous Industrial Uses: Many products and sectors depend on the unique physical and chemical properties of palladium. They include ethanol, coins, fuel production, oil refining, photography, and water treatment.

Private Investors: both individuals and investment funds buy palladium to protect portfolios against any loss that may arise due to inflammation and crises in the market. Investors buy bullion, coins, and funds that trade in metal.

What Would Make You Want To Trade in Palladium?

Is Palladium a Sure Bet Due to the Automobile Industry?

The most important market for palladium is the automobile industry. Investing in this commodity is among the ways to bet on the growing demand for automobiles in emerging markets in developing countries like India and China.

Additionally, the low-interest rate provided by the United States and Europe environments will bond well for the automobile sector. Low rates will provide affordable access to credit facilities. Because most traders finance automobile buying, rates will play a bigger role in determining the demand. Historically, the rates have remained low and as long as they remain the same, demand for vehicles and the catalytic converters that are used in them will remain high.

You Can Bet On Supply Constraints

As more than half of the world's supply of palladium comes from two nations, there is a possibility of disputes in South Africa, another major exporter of palladium, and this could disrupt supplies, leading to very high prices.

You Can Speculate on Demand Investment

As this metal is relatively new, there are few investment products made from palladium, compared to other precious metals such as silver and gold. However, as more traders know how favorable the demand and supply of this product is, the prices of palladium are bound to rise. Also, the thin liquidity in the market could exaggerate the prices.

You Can Diversify Your Portfolio

Most traders have a larger portion of their investment in stocks or bonds. Precious metals such as palladium give foundation to diversify and reduce the overall risks in your portfolio.

Should Traders Invest in Palladium?

Investors who want to trade in palladium might consider buying it together with some other commodities such as gold and silver, base metals, copper, nickel, lead and zinc, agricultural commodities such as grains, dairy products, and meats and energy. This will help traders from suffering from the volatility of an individual commodity. This will also add value through diversification to stock and portfolio.

What Trends Are Likely to Raise the Price of Palladium in the Coming Years?

Demand in China: currently, China is the largest palladium consumer globally and this may even increase in the coming years. The economy of China has seen some setbacks recently, but there are signs that this could come to an end. Therefore, investing in palladium gives you a platform to bet on a resurging Chinese economy.

Demand in Investment: the increase in ETFs has made more traders invest in precious metals. As more traders trade in gold and silver, traders are bound to seek alternative ways to trade in precious metals, and palladium could be one of the beneficiaries of this trend.

Energy Costs: the higher cost of mining can make it a very costly investment. When there is a rise in the cost of electricity and fuel, more mining companies might close or reduce their operations, and this would result in the rise in the price of palladium. However, as a trader, you must consider the risks involved in investing in palladium:

Global Recession: global recession can weaken the US and Chinese vehicle demand.

Presence of Low-Cost Substitutes: if there are cheaper substitutes for palladium, then its price will drop drastically.

Global Economic Situation or Political Uncertainty: political instability could make the US dollar strong and reduce the demand for precious metals including palladium.

How Can You Invest in Palladium?

Palladium Bullion

Investing in physical bullion like bars and coins is the major direct way to invest in palladium. However, you must know that investing in bullion will require you to have a safe storage facility. Unfortunately, the cost of setting up this facility compared to low value-to-weight could make holding physical palladium impractical.

Palladium Futures

Futures are instruments of derivatives through which investors can make leveraged bets on prices of the commodity. If there is a decline in prices, investors should deposit additional margin to maintain their positions. At expiration, the contracts will be physically settled through the delivery of physical palladium. When investing in futures, it requires sophistication of the highest level because factors like the cost of storage and interest rates could impact prices.

Palladium Options on Futures

Options are instruments of derivative that use leverage to trade in commodities. Just like futures, options have an expiration date. Also, options consist of a strike price that is the price above which the option will finish in the money.

Options traders will pay the price called a premium to buy contracts. An option bet will succeed only when the price of palladium futures rise above the strike price by a larger amount than the premium that was paid for the contract. Therefore, as an options trader, you must be right about both the size and timing of the move in futures so that you can benefit from this trade.

Palladium ETFs

ETFs are instruments of finance that trade shares on exchanges, just like stocks. ETFs Physical Palladium Shares will invest in physical palladium that it has stored in secure vaults.

Chapter 9

The Ultimate Aluminum Trading Guide

Aluminum does not occur naturally in the metallic form, but it is the most common element in the earth's crust. Aluminum is a compound of other elements. During the 19th century, Danish chemist Hans Christian Oersted was the first to extract a small amount of aluminum from ore. The complexity of aluminum made many believe that it was rarer than gold. Around the late 19th century, scientific breakthrough brought efficient and less-costly ways to extract it. Today, aluminum is found in large amounts and is used in a variety of industries and products for consumers.

How Aluminum is Made

Aluminum is produced in two methods; primary production and secondary production.

Primary Production

The production of aluminum starts with the extraction of bauxite, an ore present in the topsoil in most tropical and subtropical regions. Chemists will then form aluminum oxide, a chemical compound also known as alumina from bauxite through the Bayer process method.

For every two pounds of bauxite, you produce 1 pound of alumina. Producers will smelt aluminum through a process known as Hall-Heroult and later refine it to pure aluminum metal. You need two pounds of aluminum oxide to produce a pound of pure aluminum.

Secondary Production

This category of aluminum production involves recycling scrap aluminum metal and turning it into new aluminum. The secondary production process will require less energy than primary production, and it is environmentally friendly. The producers will extract aluminum from waste streams, then prepare for the recycling process. Aluminum will be sorted according to its chemical characteristics. A scrap containing a single composition of the chemical has more value than scrap that contains a number of alloys.

After they have sorted the aluminum, the refiners place the scrap into melting furnaces and later convert it to molten aluminum. Molten aluminum is cast into two categories of large slabs: ingots and billets. Ingots are rolled into sheet aluminum whereas billets are extruded into various shapes.

Where Does Aluminum Come From?

Aluminum producers smelt approximately 60 million metric tons a year. Primary producers from China account to more than half of the total global supply of aluminum.

Below is a list consisting of primary production of aluminum for each country.

- China: 31,400 metric tons
- Russia: 3,580 metric tons
- Canada: 3, 259 metric tons
- India: 2,750 metric tons
- United Arab Emirates: 2,400 metric tons
- Australia: 1, 680 metric tons
- Norway: 1,230 metric tons

- Bahrain: 970 metric tons
- United States of America: 840 metric tons
- Iceland: 800 metric tones

Demand for Aluminum

The major demand for aluminum is concentrated in China as a result of urbanization. Consumers in China account for about 40% of the annual global supply of aluminum. After China, Japan, the United States, and the European Union are the other largest consumers of aluminum.

Aluminum characteristics, such as being recyclable, its lime weight and resistance to corrosion make it ideal for a number of industrial uses. The below industries have the largest applications for aluminum:

Aerospace: alloys of aluminum are used to make aircraft and construct rockets.

Aluminum Cans: soda manufacturers package their products in aluminum cans as metal can quickly cool down.

Image source – Unsplash.com

Automobiles: aluminum is used to make hoods and other lime weight parts to maintain the efficiency of fuel in vehicles.

In Building and Construction: aluminum prides itself to be an energy efficient, sustainable commodity. A lot of aluminum used in construction comes from recycled materials.

Electrical: as it is an excellent conductor of electricity, it is majorly used for wiring.

In Electronics and Appliances: appliances such as refrigerators, washing machines, and laptops use aluminum.

Foil and Packaging: candies, TV dinners, and medicine packets are other items that use foil packaging.

What Impacts the Price of Aluminum?

Many global companies use aluminum in their operation, so it can be used to measure the overall health of the world economy. Below are the five major factors that drive the price of aluminum:

Demand in China

China consumes more than 40% of the annual supply of aluminum and is a major influencer of aluminum prices globally. In the last two decades, China has experienced big growth in its GDP, pushing a lot of industrial commodity prices up. Most companies in China have increased demand for aluminum, especially in the packaging sector. Also, electronics, real estate, and transportation sectors have also experienced a large demand for aluminum.

Demand in the Transportation Sector

Aluminum has the highest demand in the most developed countries in automobiles and aerospace. However, aluminum faces harsh competition from light composite materials that seek the replacement of aluminum as a constructing material. For instance, carbon fiber materials account for a large share of the aviation market. Demand for aluminum may decrease with the technological advancements of composite materials.

Demand in the Construction Industry

Markets in the construction and building sectors account for the second largest industrial demand for aluminum. In most developing countries, building materials from aluminum account for about 30% of all construction. Growth rates in construction can be volatile. Unemployment, interest rates and overall economic strength are among factors that affect the demand for aluminum and ultimately affect aluminum prices.

Input Costs

The cost involved in producing aluminum will definitely have an impact on its price. The smelting process in the production of aluminum uses a large amount of energy. When there are changes in the cost of oil or even electricity, the price of aluminum will ultimately be moved. Again, if there are large amounts of recycled aluminum, the price of the scrap metal will have a direct impact on the price of products made from aluminum.

The Value of the US Dollar

Aluminum and other precious commodities' prices are quoted in US dollar because it is a reserve currency. The prices of aluminum will remain low when the US dollar is strong and higher when the US dollar is weak.

Three Reasons for You to Invest in Aluminum

As mentioned earlier, many industries use aluminum to make products as well as for other various purposes. Therefore, trading aluminum is a means through which you can measure the growth of the manufacturing economy. The manufacturing sector represents an important portion of GDP especially in the most developing emerging economies and therefore trading in aluminum is a way to speculate on the growth of global GDP. Below are some of the best reasons to invest in aluminum:

Bet on Demand from Chinese

China is a large producer and consumer of the overall aluminum market. The fast-growing Chinese economy has required aluminum in the recent past for the construction, electronics and transportation industries, and Chinese companies supplied the metal.

However, when there was a decline in the Chinese GDP, the demand from internal industries could not accommodate the large supply, so the producers from China increased exports to other countries like the United States. This means that when there is economic growth in China, the demand for aluminum within the country will grow leading to a shortage of the commodity and ultimately higher prices.

Speculate on Demand from Transportation

The world economy depends largely on the transportation sector for growth support. A larger market for aluminum in the aerospace and automobile industries would grow when the global economy experiences expansion. People need vehicles and trucks to move to their places of work. Policies promoting growth in industrial and emerging economies could boost demand for aluminum in transportation products.

Diversifying Your Portfolio

Trading a part of your portfolio in aluminum together with other metals and commodities is a great way to diversify your assets. Baskets of commodities that include aluminum insulate investors from a decline of any particular commodity.

What are the Risks Involved in Trading Aluminum?

Investors should look at both the advantages and disadvantages of trading in aluminum, as investing in aluminum does have a fair share of challenges that may lead to its value decreasing:

Overproduction

In the recent past, China has experienced overproduction which was then dumped on the global markets. If there is no increase in demand for aluminum in China, the market might suffer from the excessive supply of aluminum.

Low Prices in Substituting Commodities

Aluminum faces high competition from composite materials. With new technological inventions has come the production of lime weight and competitively-priced commodities. If these trends go on, the price of aluminum could seriously suffer.

When the US Dollar is Strong

A strong US dollar does not occur well the prices of commodities. If the US Federal Reserve is aggressive and raises interest rates, the dollar may become strong and the prices of different commodities including aluminum will seriously suffer.

What Do Experts Say About Aluminum?

Experts have different reactions on the prospect of the future price of aluminum. Those optimistic about the commodity anchor their argument on the correlation of supply/demand imbalances globally.

For example, JPMorgan claims that reform in supply would lift markets in the future. This points to the close of smelters in China to be a positive catalyst. However, it also notes that the smelters are likely to re-open if there is a rise in the price of aluminum.

Vice president of Strategic Planning and Analysis at Alcoa Andrew Estel once said that the demand in China for aluminum would increase by 7%, which is ahead of the global rate of 5%. He said that the demand for aluminum represents 50% of the total demand for primary aluminum globally. He notes that although demand in China for aluminum would exceed the rest of the world, the surplus production in China remains an overhung on aluminum prices.

How Do You Trade In Aluminum?

Aluminum Futures

The contracts are traded globally on the CME Globex electronic trading platform. Futures are instruments of derivative through which investors can make leveraged bets on the prices of commodities. When there is a decline in prices, investors must make an additional margin to maintain the prepositions. The contracts for aluminum futures will expire on the last day of business of the contract month and are settled financially. Trading in aluminum futures needs a sophistication of the highest level because factors like the cost of storage and interest rates impacts prices.

ETFs

ETFs are financial instruments that are traded as shares on exchanges, like stocks. Currently, there are two exchange-traded funds (ETFs) that trade in aluminum futures:

- iPath Dow Jones-UBS Aluminum ETN (NYSEARCA: JJU)
- iPath Pure Beta Aluminum ETN (NYSEARCA: FOIL)
- Other ETFs generally investing in industrial metals include:
- UBS E TRACS CMCI Industrial Metals Total Return ETN (NYSEARCA: UBM)
- SPDR S&P Metals & Mining ETF (NYSEARCA: XME)

- Shares in the Mining Company

Several companies deal with mining and the processing of aluminum bauxite and ores. Although these companies do not pure-play invest in the aluminum commodity, the performance of their shares is generally related to the price of aluminum and other metals used for industrial purposes.

Five Top Aluminum Stocks by Market Capitalization

1. *Rio Tinto*: Rio Tinto has developed into the world's largest quality mines and operations.
2. *Alcoa*: Established in 1888, it is involved in increased innovation on new technologies and processes.
3. *Hydro:* a world integrated Aluminum Company
4. *Alumina Ltd:* trade in mining bauxite and refining alumina through Alcoa World Alumina & Chemicals (AWAC)
5. *Century Aluminum:* a world producer of primary aluminum. It operates aluminum facilities in the United States and Iceland.

Aluminum CFDs

This is among the easier ways of trading aluminum from the ones we have discussed. This is through a derivative instrument called contract for difference (CFD) where traders can speculate on prices of aluminum without necessarily owning aluminum, instruments of finance like ETFs, futures and options or mining shares.

Most regulated worldwide brokers give CFDs on aluminum. The clients deposit funds with the broker to serve as a margin. The advantage of trading in CFDs is that investors will be exposed to aluminum without purchasing shares, ETFs or futures. Also, it won't be necessary for investors to worry about the timing and size of markets move to profit on this trade as is the case when trading aluminum futures.

However, despite this, CFDs are high risks instruments of finance and therefore, your capital is also at risk so you will need to have enough experience as a trader or look out for a broker that gives a demo account to help you develop the knowledge before taking a risk with real money.

Chapter 10

The Ultimate Guide to Copper Trading

Copper is a commonly used metal commodity. It is a shiny, reddish-orange element that is believed to have been used by humans many years ago. In contemporary society, copper plays a big role in everyday activities. It has the same physical characteristics as silver and gold, making it suitable for a range of industrial uses, including electric wiring, roofing, industrial machinery, and plumbing.

Copper is soft, pliable, and malleable and conducts electricity and heat perfectly. The only difference copper has compared to gold and silver is that it is not used as a currency. Therefore, the price of copper is much less than other precious metals. The global supply of copper comes from underground mines and the recycling of copper products.

What are the Sources of Copper?

Underground Mines

Copper miners extract it from ore deposits found under the ground and in mines from open pits. For copper mining to be successful, it is concentrated and ground into fine materials. The copper will then be separated from waste materials and refined through a process called smelting. Although copper has been useful to humans for many years, a large percentage of the copper that has ever been mined and smelted was extracted after 1900.

Image source – Unsplash.com

The annual amount of copper mined usually exceeds 19,000,000 tons. South America leads with the most copper mines, but China is the main source of the largest producer of refined copper. Copper mines are found in most countries of the world. The countries below are the largest copper producers:

- Chile: 5,500 thousand tons
- Peru: 2,300 thousand tons
- China: 1,740thousands tons
- United States: 1,410 thousand tons
- Australia: 970 thousand tons
- Democratic Republic of Congo: 910 thousand tons
- Zambia: 740 thousand tons
- Canada: 720 thousand tons
- Russia: 710 thousand tons
- Mexico: 620 thousand tons
- Copper from Recycling

Old scrap metal converted into refined copper accounts for about 10% of the global annual copper supply and over 30% of the annual supply in the United States. Operations that includes copper smelting, brass mills, refiners and ingot makers serve as a major source of recycled copper.

Demand for copper has been steadily growing for many years due to the expansion of the global economy.

Demand for copper in developing nations has increased because their manufacturing need has also increased. The major consumers of copper are Russia, China, and Eastern Europe. They have experienced a high demand for copper and in the future, they are likely to be the determinants of copper demand. The high demand for copper comes from the following sectors:

Construction: the construction industry uses it for plumbing, electric wiring, and waterproofing of homes and commercial buildings.

Image source – Unsplash.com

Transportation Commodities: copper has perfect conductivity properties, making it an ideal choice in electric motors.

Electric Wiring and Products: due to copper's excellent electrical conductivity, it is used for integrated circuits and printed circuit boards. It is also found in vacuum tubes, cathode ray tubes, electromagnets, and magnetrons in microwave ovens.

Consumer Products and General Products: copper enjoys strong anti-microbial characteristics and the US Environmental Protection Agency approved the registration of some alloys of copper for anti-microbial materials that include bed rails, cookware, handrails, and doorknobs. Copper is also used in a lot of musical instruments.

Industrial Equipment and Machinery: copper is needed to make stills for the production of whiskey and in glassmaking, printing, and engraving equipment.

What Drives Copper Prices?

Copper has many uses in a variety of industries. This means that you can use its price as a measure of the overall strength of the global economy. Below are four major areas that represent the largest determinants of the price of copper.

Emerging Markets

As said earlier, infrastructure represents a bigger part of copper demand and emerging markets are key players in the price of copper. Fast growing economies like India and China are accumulating large portions of wealth as their economies are growing. Therefore, their need for housing and transportation infrastructure has grown, as well as other types of construction.

It is no surprise that Asia accounts for an increasing share of the global copper demand. The copper prices may greatly depend on the ability of these nations and other emerging economies such as Brazil to continue growing. A slowdown in growth in developing economies may have a negative effect on the price of copper.

US Market in Housing

The house building sector in the United States uses copper in roofing, electric wiring, fixtures in plumbing and insulation, etc. It is without a doubt that those factors that affect housing demand in US such as mortgage rates, nonfarm payrolls, demographic and US gross domestic product (GDP), all play a bigger role in determining the demand for copper. The building construction sector accounts for about half of the demand for copper in the United States. Therefore, investors should look at trends in this market to get clues concerning the future price of copper.

Disruptions in the Supply

Political situations, environmental factors, and labor-related issues can have great effects on the price of copper. South America account for a large portion of the overall copper supply, especially Peru and Chile. In the past, countries in this region have sometimes chosen governments that have nationalized the industry of mining, like Bolivia in 2007. These events can lead to disrupted supplies of copper, which in turn leads to exaggerated prices. Also, situations like workers' strikes in mines can lead to disruptions in the supply of copper which will result in higher prices.

Finally, events like earthquakes or landslides can negatively impact the production of copper. Investors in the copper mining sector should look out for geopolitical news and natural happenings that could affect the copper mining industry.

Prices of Substitution Commodities

The economic principle of substitution brings a risk of trading in any commodity, including copper. When there is a rise in the price of a certain commodity, the buyers will look for a cheaper substitute if it is available. Cheaper metal commodities like aluminum have substituted copper in power cables, electrical appliances, and refrigeration equipment. Copper competitors include lead, nickel, and iron.

Three main Reasons to Trade in Copper

Commodity traders usually refer to copper as Dr. Copper. They argue that the metal contains a Ph.D. in economics due to its price which is a dependable barometer on the overall health of the global economy. It is a fact that trading in copper will provide a way to have a bullish look at the world GDP. Below are some reasons why you might want to invest in copper.

Betting on Industrial Growth

Copper enjoys a variety of uses in the industrial sector and it's hard to build the infrastructure of a country without using it. The demand for copper is bound to rise when developing nations such as African and Asian countries and Eastern Europe modernize their economies and ultimately expand their infrastructure. As a trader who is optimistic about international growth, you should consider investing in copper.

Betting on Market in the Housing Sector

The housing market globally overheated and took a fall in the Great Recession of 2008. Traders who believe that the worst has already happened might consider having copper in their portfolios. Additionally, with more emerging markets growing, demand for housing will happen in those regions too. Copper will have the upper hand when the housing market is strong.

Speculating on Imbalance in Supply and Demand

Copper mining and copper recycling usually fall short for the demand for copper. New mines and the expansion of already existing mines may be beneficial to soak up excess demand. However, most will fear that concerns from the environment and limitations on the usage of land will keep it imbalanced for many years. Therefore, investing in copper is a way to speculate on a long term imbalance in supply and demand.

Should You Trade in Copper?

Just like any other type of investment, investing in copper comes with both advantages and disadvantages and traders should carefully weigh on these factors before investing. In the case of copper specifically, investors might want to buy the metal as a way to lower the overall risk on their portfolio. Most investors have most of their assets in the form of stocks and bonds. Investing in copper will provide a classification of assets in classes which lowers the overall portfolio volatility.

Copper is also important in providing another way to trade in the global economy, especially in the upcoming and developing industries where there is a high need for infrastructure. Trading in copper also gives a way to speculate on rebounding the housing sector in most developed economies. Copper is one of the best and most direct ways to speculate on global economic growth.

Investing in copper, however, has its fair share of risks. For example, if the global economy experiences an aggressive slowdown in economic growth, or even worse, a recession or depression, the prices of copper would indeed suffer. Also, if there are other metal substitutes for copper trading with lower prices than copper, most buyers would go for those substitutes. However, traders can mitigate the risk by purchasing a basket of industrial metals.

What Do Experts Think About Copper?

Most experts have a common belief that the great determinant of the price of copper is the economy of China in the next decade. As it is the biggest engine in developing economies, China plays a major role in determining the prices of copper. Goldman Sachs notes that high demand from China will lead to higher prices of copper in the long-term.

BMI Research Analyst for Commodities Molly Shut views the strong growing demand in China and also decelerating production supplies in Chile and China as a bullishness catalyst.

Other analysts, however, are not very optimistic about the Chinese demand story. Julius Baer analyst Carsten Menke notes that the demand in China and the recovery of the US infrastructure have been overstated and would lead to copper prices suffering.

How Do You Trade in Copper?

Copper Bullion

Traders can buy copper bullion bars as well as coins from dealers of metal in the same way they buy gold and silver bullion, and they come in different sizes. Usually, the copper grade for investment is refined to a purity level of .999 copper. Due to this purity, the prices for bullion trade at a higher price than other copper markets like futures. This premium together with the cost of storing the metal could make bullion an impractical way to invest in copper. Few dealers invest copper bullion as they do with gold bullion, but you may buy them online. Some of the online dealers for copper bullion include:

- JMBullion
- Moneymetals

Copper CFDs

Another way to trade in copper is through the use of a derivative instrument called a contract of difference (CFD). CFDs give traders an opportunity to bet on commodity prices like copper without necessarily having to own bullion of copper, ETFs, futures, mining, shares, and options.

You will know the value of a CFD by getting the difference between the copper prices at purchase and its current price. When there is an increase in the price of copper, the value of the CFD will go up and when the price of copper reduces, the value of the CFD will also reduce.

Copper Futures

These are derivative instruments that enable investors to bet on the future price of the metal.

Traders in futures will use leverage to buy contracts on an exchange. If there is a decline in prices, the investor must have the additional margin to have maintained position. Additionally, when the contract for futures is about to expire, the trader will either accept the commodity to be delivered or roll forward the position in the coming month. Trading in the futures market will require sophistication of the highest level and maintenance of active positions by the investor.

Copper Options

Another derivative instrument of investing in copper is the copper options. Just like futures, options' shelf life are limited and have an expiration date. However, unlike futures, option bets will only be successful if their prices reach a certain level before the expiry date. The traders will pay a premium to have an option in exchange for a potential payout.

For it to be successful, the price must undergo a large move to compensate the buyer of the option for the premium paid for it. This means option investors must be correct on both the size and move of the timing.

Copper ETFs

ETFs are financial instruments that trade shares on exchanges, just like stocks. There are a number of ways to invest in copper using exchange-traded funds (ETFs). Traders can buy ETFs that trade in bullion, futures, and options, or a combination of the above. Other ETFs will invest in baskets of copper mining stocks. ETFs have management fees which are passed down to the shareholders. Some of the leading copper ETFs include:

- iPath Dow Jones-UBS Copper ETN
- The United States Copper Index Fund
- iPath Pure Beta Copper ETN

Stocks of Copper

Copper investors can also trade in companies that indulge in copper mining. However, those investments are not pure players of copper. Returns from the investment will depend on other factors like how well management does and also the kind of mines that the company owns.

Furthermore, the increase in mining costs like the price of oil and equipment can sharply impact share prices. Below are some copper mining companies that you may want to invest in:

Freeport McMorant: this is the second largest copper producer globally.

BHP Billiton: an Anglo-Australian multinational natural gas company that mines metals.

Southern Copper: Headquartered in Phoenix, Arizona, it is among the major producers of copper, molybdenum, silver, zinc, gold, and lead.

Rio Tinto: an Australian-British multinational that operates in mining and metals.

Anglo-American: a major copper producer based in Johannesburg

Chapter 11

The Ultimate Guide to Lead Trading

Lead is a soft and dense metal with a low melting point. It is a component that plays an important role in the production of the battery. Additionally, due to its high density and resistance to corrosion, it is a useful commodity in industries ranging from piping to X-rays.

Lead has a history as a component dating back to ancient Egypt for the production of goods traces. During early civilizations, the metal was used in pottery grazes, paintings, piping and soldering components. At that time, ornamental objects could also be made with lead. During the 15th century, lead was used in roofing cathedrals and in the production of stained-glass windows. The late 1800s saw the invention of the lead acid storage battery. Currently, the production of lead is big business; mines produce over 4.7 million metric tons of lead annually, while metal from recycling is estimated at 6,000,000 metric tons.

How is Lead Produced?

Lead is produced using two methods: primary production which is mining and secondary production which is recycling.

Primary Production of Lead

Primary production of lead is the extraction of metal from ores located in deep underground mines. Although more than sixty minerals contain lead, only three have lead that can be mined viably.

Galena: the most common mineral extracted for the production of lead. In its pure form, it has lead and sulfur. However, Galena contains other traces of metal that include:

- Copper
- Silver
- Cadmium
- Antimony
- Arsenic

Cerussite: a mineral called white lead

Anglesite: a crystalline mineral that comes when galena is oxidized.

Over 95% of lead is extracted from any of these three minerals. However, ores that have these minerals usually contain significant deposits of other high-value metals like silver and zinc. For this, the production of lead usually happens as a byproduct of silver and zinc mining. The process of the primary production of lead involves the following three steps:

Ore Concentration

Both zinc and lead ores are found together and often have other valuable metals like silver, gold, and copper. Therefore, the very first step is to separate lead from the ores. There is a series of stages known as froth flotation that break down the ores to particles with more concentrations of lead ore.

First, the ore is ground into fine sand particles with water. The particles obtained are further diluted with water and chemical detergents and put in a series of tanks. The mixture is agitated by the tanks and both lead and zinc particles float on water whereas clay and other silicates sink at the bottom. The particles are then skimmed off the top, where they are further concentrated. A depressant which is a chemical detergent is added to the tank containing both lead and zinc particles. This will make zinc ore sink whereas lead ore will float to the top.

The lead ore will then get skimmed off while additional chemicals like copper sulfate enable zinc ores to be skimmed off later in the process. At this moment, the particles of skimmed lead will have between 40% and 80% lead. The other portion of the concentration will have particles like sulfur, silver or zinc. The particles can now be heated in smelters.

Smelting Process

To remove sulfur and other impurities, the particles of lead are mixed with other materials that include lime and sandstone. The mixture that will come is spread on moving grate and heated by air, reaching 2,550 degrees. The roasting process will produce a brittle material known as sinter, which is mainly lead oxide but may also contain iron, zinc and silicon oxides. The sulfur present in the concentrate will burn away in the form of sulfur dioxide gas.

Sinter is broken into lamps and later loaded to a blast furnace containing coke fuel. The coke will then burn at 2,200 degrees and produce a molten lead.

Refining Process

The molten lead will produce lead base bullion that is 95-99% pure. It is then further refined in drossing kettles to remove any additional impurities. For it to be viable commercially, the lead must be 99-99.999% pure. After impurities are removed and the lead is cooled, it is put in blocks that can weigh a maximum of a ton. Refining companies produce lead alloys for specific industrial uses.

Secondary Production

This process involves recycling items like batteries. Other items such as pipes, sheets, cable coverings, and other metals can also be recycled to get lead. Lead recycling is very simple and accounts for almost half of the total production of lead. In both the US and Europe, the rate of recycling of lead from batteries is 99 percent.

Smelters will separate the components of batteries like the paste, lead, and electrolytes. The particles of lead are processed in blast furnaces, refined, and used for new batteries. The quality of lead obtained from recycling is the same as the one that will be obtained from mining.

China is the leading country in mine production and accounts for more than half of the total output. This is more than five times the second largest producer, Australia.

What are the Top Ten Lead-Producing Countries?

- China: 2,400,000 thousand metric tons
- Australia: 500,000 thousand metric tons
- United States: 335,000 thousand metric tons
- Peru: 310,000 thousand metric tons
- Mexico: 250,000 thousand metric tons
- Russia: 225,000 thousand metric tons
- India: 135,000 thousand metric tons
- Bolivia: 80,000 thousand metric tons
- Sweden: 76,000 thousand metric tons
- Turkey: 75,000 thousand metric tons

According to United States Geological Survey (USGS), these are the reserves for each country:

- Australia: 35,000 thousand metric tons
- China: 17,000 thousand metric tons
- Russia: 6,400 thousand metric tons
- Peru: 6,300 thousand metric tons
- Mexico: 5,600 thousand metric tons

What are the Main Uses of Lead?

Lead is a malleable and dense metal. It also has a low melting point, is resistant to corrosion and is able to absorb radiation. Therefore, many sectors depend on it to make their products. Below are the four main uses of lead:

Ammunition: the physical characteristics of lead make it favorable to produce bullets.

Image source – Pixabay.com

Batteries: the chemical characteristics of lead make it anchor batteries and storage technologies for renewable energy sources.

Industrial Parts and Sheets: industrial sheets made from lead reduce noise and vibration.

Protective Shielding: lead is able to absorb electromagnetic radiation effectively. This makes it important to create shields in particle accelerators, X-ray equipment, and containers that transport radioactive materials.

What Drives the Price of Lead?

Demand in China

China alone uses more than 40% of the global annual supply of lead, so it's no doubt that it will play a bigger role in driving the prices of lead. The growth in Chinese GDP in the last two decades have pushed the prices of many commodities higher. However, in the recent past, Chinese GDP has slowed down, leading to doubts concerning the future demand for metals, including lead. Lead prices largely depend on demand from China for both batteries and devices for power storage.

If there is growth in industrialization and urbanization in China, demand for power sources will increase and ultimately lead to increased prices for lead. Investors should be keen on the power consumption in China to have clues on the future price of lead.

Global Stocks

London Metal Exchange (LME) keeps track of the global lead stock level and investors should follow the data carefully.

Movement in these stock numbers could be an indicator of a shortage in supply or guts. Any drop in the global stocks will lead to a price increase, whereas the increase in stocks will lead to oversupply which will result in a reduction of prices.

Demand Outlook

An excellent analysis of lead must focus on the battery sector that accounts to over 85% of all lead demand. Data from the government from both the upcoming and most developed countries shows that demand for energy might double in the next ten years.

China and India have begun trading in smart grid technology so that they can meet this demand. These investments have led to an expansion in the usage of lead-acid batteries in both electric and hybrid vehicles.

There were environmental concerns in 2011 that led to reduced production of lead batteries, although today the production is on the rise again. New applications like the grid storage to generate renewable energy could drive increased demand for lead-acid batteries. If there is an increase in the demand for these technologies, prices of lead could further go up.

Substitute Technologies

Lead-acid batteries get stiff competition from substitute technologies such as lithium-ion batteries as a source of power storage and most experts in the industry believe that lithium-ion batteries could effectively substitute lead batteries in many automotive applications. However, there are some limitations to using a lithium-ion battery, as lead-acid batteries work better in vehicles that involve high power. Additionally, lithium-ion batteries are relatively expensive.

Investors ought to monitor this and any other competitor of lead-acid batteries. If there are improvements to those competitors, the prices of lead are bound to suffer.

Concerns in Health

Many studies have shown that long-term exposure to lead is toxic. Due to this, there has been the removal of lead in products like paints, drinking water pipes, and gasoline. If there is any more evidence to confirm the harmful effects of lead exposure, consumers may pick other alternatives.

Reasons to Invest in Lead

Speculate on Demand in Automobile

The most crucial market for lead manufacturers is the automobile market. Trading in lead might be a way to speculate on the increasing demand for automobiles in developing markets like India and China. Again, the availability of low interest rates in both the United States and Europe will bode well for the car-making industry. Low rates would lead to affordable access to credit markets. Since most individuals finance their automobile purchases, the rates might play a crucial role in determining demand. If the rates remain as low as they have been in the past, demand for vehicles and batteries will remain strong.

Hedge against Inflation and Weak US Dollar

Trading in lead is a way to speculate on high inflation and weak US dollar. Lead is priced in US dollar, so the American economy can affect its price. The US Federal Reserve Bank has seen low-interest rates and a weak US dollar for a couple of years.

This trend is likely to go on and support consumer spending and borrowing which will be beneficial to the price of lead. A weak US dollar could lead to inflation. The lead is in limited supply, so its supply depends majorly on the recycling of batteries and other items. The price of this commodity could benefit from concerns of inflation.

Diversification of Portfolios

Most investors will put the majority of their assets in stocks and bonds. Commodities like lead will give investors a way to diversify and minimize the risk in their portfolios.

How Can You Invest in Lead?

Traders have limited options for access to Lead Prices:

Lead Futures

Futures are derivative instruments that allow traders to make leveraged speculation on the prices of commodities. When there is a decline in prices, investors will put additional margin to maintain positions. When they expire, the contracts are settled physically through delivery.

Trading in futures needs a sophistication of the highest level because factors like the cost of storage and interest rates can affect prices.

Lead ETFs

These are financial instruments that invest in shares on exchanges, just like stocks do. Currently, two ETFs trade in lead futures:

- iPath Pure Beta Lead ETN
- iPath Dow Jones-AIG Lead ETN

Company Shares for Lead

There are no publicly owned companies that purely invest in lead. A lot of the production of lead comes as a byproduct of mining other commodities like zinc and silver.

Vedanta: a globally diversified company that majors in zinc, silver, lead, iron, aluminum, copper, ore, power, oil and gas.

Southern Copper Corporation: SCC is among the largest integrated producers of copper in the world. It deals with the production of lead, zinc, copper, coal, molybdenum, and silver. Its facilities are situated in Peru and Mexico and they undergo exploration activities in these nations as well as in Chile.

Glencore: an Australian company that is a leading integrated producer and marketer of the commodity.

CFDs

Another way to trade in lead is with the use of a contract for difference (CFD) instrument of the derivative. You will get the value of a CFD through the difference between the lead price at the time of buying and its current price. Most regulated brokers in the world give CFDs on lead, and clients deposit funds with the broker to serve as a margin. The good thing with CFDs is that they allow investors to get exposed to prices of lead without purchasing shares, futures, ETFs or options.

Chapter 12

Guide to Trading Nickel

Why Nickel is valuable

Nickel is a solid, lustrous, silver-like white metal. It is strong, magnetic, ductile and corrosion-resistant, and has a high melting point and catalytic characteristics. All these favorable characteristics make nickel among one of the most used metals for industrial purposes.

Production of Nickel

The supply of nickel comes from two sources: primary production which is mining and secondary production which is recycling. Mining gives most of the supply, although USGS notes that the quantity recovered from recycling in the US represent 43% of the total usage.

Primary Production

Nickel comes from two kinds of ores, sulfidic and lateritic. Each kind has specific properties that relate to how it is mined. Ore processing and separation of nickel from the ores is also dependent on the type of ore.

Although sulfidic mining is more expensive, separating them from the ores is less costly than nickel extraction from lateric deposits. Also, sulfidic ores have other valuable minerals that could be extracted when nickel is being produced.

Secondary Production

A small amount of nickel is produced to its actual original state; instead, scrap items are recycled into economically viable materials that contain nickel. For instance, it is usually not valuable to extract nickel from products made from stainless steel. However, when these products are recycled, it allows manufacturers to make other new stainless steel products that contain nickel.

The largest nickel mining country in the world is the Philippines. However, no one single country has taken dominance of the production of nickel, as its mining happens in many different geographical regions and countries. Below are the top ten nickel-mining countries:

- Philippines: 500,000 thousand metric tons
- Russia: 256,000 thousand metric tons
- Canada: 255,000 thousand metric tons
- Australia: 206,000 thousand metric tons
- New Caledonia: 205,000 thousand metric tons
- Indonesia: 168,000 thousand metric tons
- Brazil: 142,000 thousand metric tons
- China: 90,000 thousand metric tons
- Guatemala: 58,600 thousand metric tons
- Cuba: 56,000 thousand metric tons
- Countries with the Largest Nickel Reserves:
- Australia: 19,000 thousand metric tons
- Brazil: 10,000 thousand metric tons
- Russia: 7,600 thousand metric tons

- New Caledonia: 6,700 thousand metric tons
- Cuba: 5,500 thousand metric tons

What are the Main Uses of Nickel?

Electronics: alloys of nickel and iron are mainly used in electronics.

Image source – Pixabay.com

Stainless Steel: almost 2/3 of the total nickel produced is used in stainless steel. Austenitic steel is a good example of a type of stainless steel that contains a significant amount of nickel. Many items contain austenitic steel, including cookware, automotive trim, food and beverage equipment, cutlery, industrial equipment, chemical, mining, and cryogenic among others.

Catalysts: nickel plays an important role in a lot of catalysts that facilitate chemical reactions.

Plating: electro nickel-plating uses electric current to cover conductive metals with a nickel coating.

Rechargeable Batteries: nickel is an important component in rechargeable battery systems in electronics, transportation, power tools, and emergency power supplies.

What are the Drivers of Nickel Prices?

The following factors mainly drive the price of nickel:

Demand in China

China accounts for over half of the global annual demand for nickel. Ten years ago, China accounted for only 20% of the total global demand.

The rapid development of the Chinese economy over the past ten years has actually accounted for the increased consumption. However, due to a slowing down of the Chinese GDP in the recent past, doubts have risen about the future demand for nickel and other metals used for industrial purposes. Ultimately, the price of nickel is largely dependent on demand from China for all items from stainless steel products to batteries. If both industrialization and urbanization renew their high rate of growth, the price of nickel will also rise. Therefore, investors must always look out for data on the Chinese economy to have clues on the price of nickel.

Global Stocks

Traders should follow inventory levels kept by London Metals Exchange (LME) for nickel and other metals to learn about either the shortness or increased supply of nickel. If the levels in the inventory are low, then the market may be experiencing a shortage of supply of nickel. This could automatically lead to increased prices. Similarly, if there is a lot of stockpile and the expansion of inventory levels, the market might experience an oversupply of the commodity, leading to lower prices.

Nickel investors particularly keep a close look at inventories from China because they have the greatest impact on the prices of nickel. Information on shipping containers coming to China gives valuable clues concerning the demand for all metal commodities including nickel.

World Demand Outlook

General economic activity specifically in the industrial area impacts the demand for nickel. Another market segment that deserves close attention is the use of nickel to make stainless steel alloys used for building activities. Alloys of stainless steel and nickel produce durable structures and protect them against corrosion. A perfect example of a project that used nickel is the construction of the Great Bridge in China. In the recent past, the US has not been involved in major infrastructure projects. If it does, the price of nickel will definitely rise. Similarly, if other developed countries indulge in replacing their infrastructure, nickel prices are bound to rise.

Government Policies

Some government policies could impact the price of nickel. In the past, Indonesia has been a major exporter of nickel. However, in the recent past, the government has banned the exportation of laterite ore. The reason for this ban from the government was among efforts to promote the smelting industry in the country. Lately, there has been a resumption in exports due to budget deficits in the country.

The Philippines, the largest miner of nickel has threatened to end mining operations in the country. Situations such as this one in the Philippines or involving other governments can have a major impact on both the supply and price of nickel.

Input Costs

Nickel is found in ore bodies, and the breaking down of ore bodies to extract nickel requires energy. Nickel production requires large supplies of electricity, coal and crude oil. Both mines and blast furnaces use energy to extract nickel ores from the ground and to process it to nickel. All these costs can have a large impact on the primary production of nickel. The cost of the scrap can similarly have a big impact on the cost of the secondary output.

Reasons to Invest in Nickel

Traders should invest in nickel for the following reasons:

Speculating on Stainless Steel Demand

Expansion in the global demand for stainless steel products could lead to a rise in nickel prices.

China, for example, continues with the urbanization and industrialization of its economy. Tanks, buildings, mining & industrial equipment, and bridges are just among the many applications that require nickel.

Also, the United States will soon embark on infrastructure for a number of years to come. Railways, bridges, and airports in the US are among projects that need upgrading. All these activities will need engineering resources and nickel will be highly needed to build many of these projects.

Hedge against Inflation and Weak US Dollar

Trading in nickel is a way to speculate on a weak US dollar and inflation. Since nickel is priced in US dollar, the American economy can have a huge impact on its price. The United States Federal Reserve Bank has ensured that interest rates and the US dollar remain low for a long time. The bankers in the Central Bank are likely to maintain this trend in order to support both consumer borrowing and spending. These will be beneficial to the price of nickel and other commodities.

A weak dollar could signal inflation concerns. There is a shortage in the supply of nickel and its production is an energy consuming endeavor. The price of nickel and other commodities are likely due to inflation concerns.

Diversification of Portfolio

Most investors have a large part of their assets in stocks and bonds. Commodities like nickel will give traders a way to diversify and minimize the general risk in their portfolios.

How to Invest in Nickel

Traders have many ways to get exposed to prices of nickel:

Nickel Bullion

The most direct way to invest in nickel is with the use of physical nickel bullion. However, when you trade in nickel bullion, you must have a safe storage facility. Therefore, the cost of storage together with the low value-to-weight ratio makes holding physical nickel impractical. It is interesting that the American nickel coin contains only 25% nickel and 75% copper.

Nickel futures

LME trades in contracts of nickel with a minimum of 99.80% purity. Each contact has six metric tons of nickel and is priced in dollars.

Futures are derivative instruments through which investors make leveraged speculation on prices of the commodity. If there is a decline in the prices, investors will deposit additional margin to maintain their positions. During expiration, the contracts are settled by delivering the metal.

Trading in futures requires sophistication of the highest level because factors like cost of storage and interest rates could impact prices.

Option for Nickel on Futures

Options are derivative instruments that use leverage to trade in commodities. Just like futures, options have an expiry date. Options, however, contain a strike price which refers to the price above which the option will finish in the money.

Buyers of options will pay an amount called premium to buy the contracts. Option speculation will succeed only when the future price of nickel rises above the strike price above the premium paid for the contract. Therefore, for investors of options to benefit from their trades, they must be right about the size and timing of the move of nickel futures.

Nickel ETFs

ETFs are financial instruments that trade as shares on exchanges, just like stocks. There are currently two exchange-traded funds (ETFs) that trade in nickel futures:

- iPath Dow Jones AIG Nickel Ga

- iPath Pure Beta Nickel ETN

Nickel Shares in Companies

Many publically traded companies have exposure to prices of nickel. Just as trading in companies is a leveraged way to have exposure to prices of nickel, a lot of these companies have significant exposure to prices of other metals and commodities. Additionally, factors like company management and the general stock market can impact these investments.

Glencore: an international trading and mining company.

Pure Nickel: it engages in the acquisition, exploration, and development of mineral characteristics in Canada.

BHP: an Anglo-Australian multinational mining, metal and natural gas Company.

CFDs

Another way to invest in nickel is by using a contract for difference (CFD) derivative instrument. CFD gives traders an opportunity to bet on nickel prices. The value of the CFD is obtained by finding the difference between the cost of a nickel at buying time and its current price.

Chapter 13

The Ultimate Guide In Zinc Trading

Why Zinc is Valuable

Zinc is a bluish-white element that can be refined into metal. It is corrosion-resistant, so it is ideal in galvanizing iron and steel. Zinc produces brass which is a zinc alloy containing between 55% and 95% copper. Zinc was discovered as an element in 1746 by a German chemist called Sigismund Marggraf. However, it was used long before this during the early civilizations. Ancient miners in Asia smelted Zinc in India in the 9th century. During the rule of the Roman Empire, soldiers used copper and zinc to make brass weapons.

Currently, mining of zinc in the world exceeds 11.9 million metric tons a year. There are zinc mines in over fifty countries and the metal produced plays an important role in the steel industry.

Zinc Production

Primary Production

Over 80% of zinc is mined from under the ground. Surface mining accounts to only about 8% of all mining, whereas mines using both methods account for 12%. Ores containing zinc include zinc sulfide (sphalerite), zinc silicate (calamine), zinc carbonate (smithsonite), and both manganese and iron compounds called franklinite. Zinc and lead usually come together and contain valuable metals like silver, gold, and copper. The primary production of zinc involves four steps:

Ore concentration: Ore concentration involves a series of steps known as froth floatation aimed at breaking down ores into particles with high levels of zinc. At the start, the ore is ground into fine powder and then put in flotation tanks that contain water, chemicals and pine oil. Filters are used to remove water and oils leaving behind a mixture that looks like a paste. The mixture is then mixed with lime and roasted in temperatures of 2,500 degrees Fahrenheit leading to the production of solid mass – zinc oxide.

Smelting: In this second step, high – powered furnaces help in breaking down zinc oxide into zinc element.

Refining: At this stage, iron and other impurities settle at the bottom, whereas pure zinc remains at the top.

Alloying: Large amounts of zinc are used as alloys. Refiners re-melt zinc and then combine it with exact amounts depending on the application while making alloys.

Secondary Production

Zinc recycling is a viable economic activity. In the USA, almost 35,000 tons of zinc are recycled in a year. Recycling includes materials such as zinc oxide from blast furnaces and the residue obtained from the process of zinc galvanizing with steel.

China leads in the mining of zinc, producing about 40% of its total annual supply.

What are the Top Ten Mining Countries?

- China: 4,500 thousand metric tons
- Peru: 1,300 thousand metric tons
- Australia: 850 thousand metric tons
- United States: 780 thousand metric tons

- Mexico: 710 thousand metric tons
- India: 650 thousand metric tons
- Bolivia: 460 thousand metric tons
- Kazakhstan: 340 thousand metric tons
- Canada: 310 thousand metric tons
- Sweden: 250 thousand metric tons
- Which Counties Have the Most Zinc Reserves?
- Australia: 63,000 thousand metric tons
- China: 40,000 thousand metric tons
- Peru: 25,000 thousand metric tons
- Mexico: 17,000 thousand metric tons
- United States: 11,000 thousand metric tons

Almost a third of all zinc produced is used to galvanize other metals like steel and iron. However, zinc has other many uses, including:

Making Alloys: zinc is combined with other metals to form strong alloys. Brass, nickel, aluminum, and silver are some of the alloys of zinc. Some musical instruments and hardware items use brass in construction, whereas item like pipes and electrical items use solder.

Galvanizing Material: galvanizing steel and iron help prevent them from rusting and corrosion. The most common way to galvanize steel is through electroplating. Items such as lamp posts, safety barriers, car bodies, and lamp posts use galvanized steel.

Zinc Oxide: manufacturers of many products prefer using zinc oxide to make their products. They include; textiles, electrical equipment, cosmetics pharmaceuticals, rubber, paints, soaps, and others.

Die Castings: this involves producing metal parts with the use of molds. The automobile, hardware, and electrical industries use zinc for die-casting parts.

Zinc Sulfide: zinc sulfide plays an important role in making products such as X-ray screens, luminous paints, and fluorescent lights.

What Drives Zinc Prices?

The following factors mainly drive the price of zinc:

Chinese Demand

Just like any other commodity, zinc is affected by China in determining its price. China is a major consumer of refined zinc used in galvanizing steel. This means that the demand for steel is an important indicator of zinc demand in China and in any other country. Decisions on whether to roll out infrastructure projects or stall them can create great changes in the demand for steel. In the end, these decisions will also affect the demand for zinc.

Money policies in the People's Bank of China are among the major factors that will affect the demand for zinc and steel. Stimulating policies can lead to an increased demand for these commodities, while tougher measures could decrease demand.

Supply from China

A significant factor affecting the output of zinc in China is the country's increased environmental awareness. Having poor air quality has made the government take hard measures in the mining industry because they view it as a contributor to pollution. If the country reaches a point where it decides to curb zinc mining as a way to deal with this problem, then the state will depend on imports, leading to a shortage in supply. In turn, this could lead to an increase in the price of zinc.

Global Stocks

London Metal Exchange (LME) keeps global tracks on stock levels for zinc and other commodities. Investors follow these keenly for clues concerning a shortage or increase in supplies. When inventory levels drop, the market could face a shortage of zinc supply in the following days. This could mean higher prices for the commodity. Similarly, if there is a lot of stockpiling and inventory levels increase, the market could face an oversupply of the commodity leading to lower prices.

Demand in the USA

There is an increased demand for galvanized steel in construction and infrastructure. The US has not invested in infrastructure for many years now. If the government embarks on other infrastructure projects, the price of steel could rise. This is likely to create demand for zinc, leading to higher prices. A strong US economy will lead to increased demand for automobiles. The transportation sector is a reliable measure for demand on galvanized steel and ultimately increases demand for zinc.

Input Costs

Zinc comes in ore bodies, and to extract elements, they require a lot of energy. Both the mining and refining of zinc needs adequate supplies of electricity, coal and crude oil. This cost could lead to big impacts on the primary production of zinc. Similarly, the price of scrap can have a secondary effect on zinc.

Traders might consider investing in zinc for the following reasons:

Bet on Strong Global Economy

If there is a rise in demand for zinc alloys, galvanized steel, and other steel products, the prices could go higher. For this to happen, China must resume its growth trend. China has experienced a slowdown in the past, but there are signs that the economy might be strengthening again. Basically, trading in zinc is a way to speculate on the resurging economy of China.

Another catalyst for high zinc prices is the growing United States economy. The demand for galvanized steel for the infrastructure and automobile industries in the US could also lead to higher prices.

A Hedge Against Weak US Dollar and Inflation

Trading in zinc is a way to speculate on inflation and on the weak US dollar. Zinc is priced in dollars, so the US economy can have a great impact on its price. Central bankers in the US keeps interest rates low to support consumer spending and borrowing. These conditions positively impact zinc prices.

A weak US dollar could lead to inflation concerns. The supply of zinc is limited and producing it requires a lot of energy. The price of zinc is likely to respond positively to inflation fears.

Diversifying Your Portfolio

Most investors have the majority of their assets in bonds and stocks. Commodities like zinc could give traders a way to expand and decrease the overall risk in their portfolio.

How Do You Invest in Zinc?

Zinc Bullion

Physical zinc bullion like the ingots is the major direct way to trade in zinc. However, trading in bullion requires a secure storage system. The cost of this storage and the low value-to-weight ratio makes it impractical to hold.

Zinc Futures

The Chicago Mercantile Exchange gives a contract on zinc at 25 metric tons. The contracts are traded globally on the CME Globex electronic platform and have different expiration months. Futures are derivative instruments by which investors make leveraged speculations on the prices of commodities. If there is a decline in prices, investors are to deposit additional margin to maintain their positions. At expiration, the contracts are physically settled by delivering zinc.

Investing in futures requires a sophistication of the highest level because factors like the cost of storage and interest rates impact on prices.

Zinc ETFs

These are financial instruments that trade like shares on exchanges, just like stocks.

Shares of Zinc Companies

Many publicly traded companies have exposure to prices of zinc. These companies give traders a way to gain exposure to prices of zinc and other metals as well as prices of commodities. Additionally, factors like company management and the general stock market can also have an impact on these investments:

Teck Resources: a Canadian mining company involved in exploring and developing mining projects globally. The production of zinc represents a larger portion of the profit.

Hecla Mining: a US mining company dealing with base and precious metals. It engages in the acquisition, exploration, and development of mineral characteristics globally.

Hudbay Minerals: a Canadian integrated mining company that focuses on producing precious and base metals in both North and South America.

CFDs

CFDs allow investors to bet on zinc prices. The price of a CFD is the value difference between zinc prices during purchasing time and the current price. Some regulated brokers give CFDs on zinc. Clients will deposit funds with the broker to serve as a margin. The good thing with trading in CFDs is that they give you exposure to prices of zinc without necessarily purchasing shares, ETFs, futures or options.

Chapter 14

Ultimate Guide on Trading Steel

Steel is among the most important metals used globally in both the engineering and construction sectors. It is an alloy that largely contains iron and little amounts of silicon, manganese, sulfur, phosphorous and oxygen.

How Does Production of Steel Happen?

Steel is produced in furnaces by use of three different ways:

Blast Furnace – Basic Oxygen Furnace (BF – BOF): This is a method that uses iron core, some recycled steel and coal. Iron ore is then reduced to iron and later converted to steel in the blast furnaces. The makers of steel will then cast and roll the steel and subsequently deliver it in the form of plates, coils, sections or bars. The BF – BOF method account to over 75 percent of the total steel production globally.

Electric Arc Furnace (EAF): This is a method that mostly uses recycled steel and electric power. However, it sometimes uses various sources of metallic iron. Electricity is used to melt recycled steel EAFs and accounts for almost 25percent of total steel produced globally.

Open Heart Furnace (OHF): this method uses an intensive amount of energy and is unfriendly to the environment. OHF accounts for less than 0.5 percent of the total steel produced globally.

The total production of steel globally is more than 1.600 million metric tons in a year. Production of steel happens from different regions globally, but recently it has dramatically shifted from Western countries to China. Steel producers from China now account for about half of the supply of steel globally.

Which Countries Have a Considerable Amount of Steel?

- China: 808.4 million metric tons
- Japan: 104.8 million metric tons
- India: 95.6 million metric tons
- USA: 78.5: million metric tons
- Russia: 70.8 million metric tons
- South Korea: 68.6 million metric tons
- Germany: 42.1 million metric tons
- Turkey: 33.2 million metric tons
- Brazil: 31.3 million metric tons
- Ukraine: 24.2 million metric tons

Demand for steel has risen steadily in the recent past as developing countries have increased their need for infrastructure. China consumes about 45% of the annual production of steel while other countries in Asia consume almost 17%. Europe accounts for about 10% of the total demand for steel annually, whereas NAFTA accounts for 9% of its usage.

Main Uses of Steel

Infrastructure and Construction: Engineers and building personnel use steel to construct high-rise buildings, residential buildings, rail lines, industrial shades, and many more structures. Infrastructure accounts to over nearly half of the annual usage of steel in a year.

Image source – Pixabay.com

Metal products: This industry includes consumer goods like washing machines, air conditioners, and refrigerators. It accounts for nearly 11% of the annual demand for steel.

Mechanical tools and automotive industry: Sheets of steel are used for hoods, mufflers, doors, vehicle frames, and fuel tanks. This industry accounts for about 30% of the demand for steel.

Electrical Equipment: This industry accounts for about 3% of the global steel demand and includes connectors, component brackets and other equipment.

Domestic Appliances: Cookware, knives and other kitchen appliances use steel.

What Affects the Price of Steel?

Different industries in the world use steel to make their products. This means that steel can be used as a perfect barometer for strength in the global economy. Below are the greatest factors that impact the price of steel:

Chinese Economy

China alone consumes almost half of the annual supply of steel globally and, so it may be a significant determinant of prices of steel.

China has experienced a double-digit growth over the past couple of years creating a robust increase in the demand for steel in building offices, in residential housing and many other construction types.

However, it is worth noting that China is also a major steel exporter. Having that Chinese growth has slowed trajectory, its demand for steel has decreased. As a result, producers of steel from China have flooded the international market with low-cost steel exports leading to depressed prices.

Generally, when China has strong internal demand, it will lead to higher prices of steel, whereas when it experiences weak demand, it will lead to oversupply and ultimately low prices. Other countries such as Brazil and India will at a lesser extent affect the prices of steel.

Global Demand for Infrastructure

Both construction and infrastructure account for a huge percentage of demand for steel. Developed economies like the United States and Europe are planning to embark on large-scale infrastructure projects aimed at replacing crumbling airports, bridges, and other transportation systems. The rise in demand for steel in such infrastructure projects will undoubtedly impact on the prices of steel, making them rise.

Demand in Transportation

Demand for trains, ships, and cars can drive the price of steel. When the global economy is doing well, demand for ships and trains to transport cargo will also grow. Likewise, a strong economy will create high consumer demand for cars. The transport sector is ultimately a reliable barometer for the economy generally and therefore a strong economy will lead to prices of steel going up, whereas when the economy is weak, the costs of steel will be depressed.

Input Costs

The two main materials used in producing steel is iron and scrap metal. Emerging economies such as India, Brazil and China account for a larger portion of the supply of these materials globally and also produce large amounts of steel in their industries. Both the availability and the price of this materials is largely dependent on the size of internal demand in these countries.

Another significant input cost while making steel is the cost of energy since a lot of heat is required in melting the iron ore.

Costs of Substitutes

Due to advancements in technology, there has been the production of durable composite materials that can substitute steel. A good example is the carbon fibers reinforced polymers that have properties that include strong strength-to-weight ratios making them suitable substitute for steel in many uses. If the improvements for composite technologies goes further, demand for steel could drop.

Reasons You Could Invest in Steel

Steel is globally used in production so you can use its demand as a reliable indicator of the strength of the manufacturing sector. Manufacturing plays an important role in the economy, so trading in steel is a way to have a bullish view on the growth of world GDP. The main reasons to invest in steel are the following:

Speculate on Large Infrastructure Programs

The amount of steel used to build bridges, airports, and railways exceeds the amount needed in other applications. In many years, the

US has not invested in infrastructure projects. Should it resume these projects, the price of steel would definitely rise. Similarly, when developing countries improve their infrastructure, the price of steel also rises.

Speculate on developing markets demand

The rising demand for infrastructure in developing countries like China has been instrumental in increasing the demand for steel. Traders who are interested in participating in the growth of developing markets without trading in stock markets of the concerned countries should think about trading in steel.

Speculate on Demand in Transportation

The global economy is dependent on transportation for growth. Ships offer transportation services internationally, whereas trucks and trains transport goods across countries. Again, people need these transport systems to travel from one place to the other. Policies promoting the industrial sector in developing economies should increase steel demand.

How to Invest in Steel

Investors have many ways to invest in this commodity:

Steel Futures

Futures are derivative instruments that allow traders to make leveraged bets on the price of a commodity. If there is a reduction in prices, investors should deposit additional margins to have maintained positions. Steel futures expire on the business day before the last Wednesday of the contract's month. At expiration, the contracts are settled financially. Factors like cost of storage and interest rates can impact future prices and sophistication of the highest level is required.

Steel Options

Options are derivative instruments that use leverage to trade in commodities. Just like futures, options have an expiry date. However, options contain a strike price that is the price above which the option will finish in the money. The buyer of the option will pay an amount called a premium to buy contacts. A bet will be considered successful only if the steel price goes above the amount strike by an amount exceeding the premium paid for the contract. This means that options investors must be correct about the size and timing of steel to benefit from their trades in the future.

ETFs

ETFs are financial instruments that trade like shares on exchanges, just like stocks. Currently, there is one steel exchange that purely trades in companies that produce steel.

• VanEck Vectors Steel ETF

Shares in Steel Companies

There are many companies that deal with mining and processing iron ore or the production of steel. Although these companies are not purely investing in steel, their share performance is related to its general price.

Rio Tinto: a UK metal company dealing with processing and marketing mineral resources.

Vale: a Brazilian company that produces and sells iron ore to make steel.

BHP Billiton: Australian company dealing with acquiring, developing and marketing natural resources globally.

Cleveland - Cliffs Inc.: a US company engaging in mining and natural resources.

CFDs

Another way to trade in steel is with the use of a contract for difference (CFD) derivative instrument. CFDs allows investors to bet on the price of steel company shares.

Conclusion

Since historical times, most metals, especially gold and silver, have been viewed as valuable items. Even today, metals have a special place in an investor's portfolio. You must do a good observation to determine what metals to invest in, as well as their volatility.

Metal trading give an essential and effective way to expand your portfolio. The secret in achieving success with this trading is to know your goals and risk profile before starting. The volatility of metals can be harnessed in to increase wealth, but when not checked, it can result in ruins. As a trader, you should be keen on some of the major issues that we have highlighted in this book and information from other sources so that you can stay up-to-date with the current trends in this trade. By doing this, you will be able to achieve more as a trader.

Printed in Great Britain
by Amazon

35687976R00086